DISCOVERING
THE
Magic
OF
Christmas

DISCOVERING THE Magic OF Christmas

75 WAYS TO MAKE YOUR HOLIDAY MORE MEANINGFUL

Heather Holm

CFI
Springville, Utah

ISBN 13: 978-1-59955-182-1

Published by CFI, an imprint of Cedar Fort, Inc., 2373 W. 700 S., Springville, UT 84663
Distributed by Cedar Fort, Inc. www.cedarfort.com

LIBRARY OF CONGRESS CATALOGING-IN-PUBLICATION DATA

Holm, Heather, 1956-
    Discovering the magic of Christmas : 75 ways to make your holiday more meaningful / Heather Holm.
        p. cm.
    ISBN 978-1-59955-182-1
    1. Christmas decorations. 2. Handicraft. I. Title.

TT900.C4H68 2008
745.594'12--dc22

200801478

Cover design by Nicole Williams
Cover design © 2008 by Lyle Mortimer

Printed in the United States of America

10 9 8 7 6 5 4 3 2 1

Printed on acid-free paper

I will always be proud of you, Kev.

Table of Contents

Acknowledgments xi

Introduction xii

1. Organize Yourself 1

2. It's Time to Decorate 3
Simple Cross-stitch Ornaments 3
Felt Christmas Tree Ornaments... 11
Old-fashioned Salt Dough Ornaments 12
Plaster of Paris Ornaments... 12
Beaded Ornaments
    Chenille Pipe Cleaner and Beads Ornaments 14
    Crystal Icicle Ornament 15
    Crystal Loop Ornament 16
    Bead and Sequin Styrofoam Ball Ornaments 17
Faux Stained Glass Ornaments and Decorations 18
Advent Calendar..22
Garlands
    Bead Garland..25
    Macaroni Garland 25
    Popcorn Garland 26
Homemade Candles 26
Tissue Paper Christmas Wreath...27
Snow Globes...28
Mini Christmas Stockings...29

3. Once upon a Time 31
Suggested Movies 31
Suggested Books and Short Stories 35

4. Greetings to a Friend 39
Embossing 39
Glitter 40
Scrapbooking Cards 41
Greeting Card Holder 47

5. Simple Gift Ideas 48
Homemade Gift Boxes 48
Gift Baskets 51
    Cookies and Cocoa Gift Basket 51
    Crackers and Cheese Gift Basket 52
Ice Melter in a Bucket 52
Bath Salts 53
Heating Pad 54
Homemade Candles 54
Advent Calendar 54
Oven Mitt and Poems 54
Refrigerator Magnets 56
Snow Globes 56
Handmade Ornaments 56
Family Cookbook 56
Family Photo Calendar 56
Children's Handprints 57
Personalized Towels 57
Personalized Pillows and Pillowcases 57
Handmade Jewelry 57
Family Histories 57
Candy Bar Wrappers 58
Additional Gift Suggestions 58

6. Wrap It Up 64
Homemade Wrapping Paper 64
Homemade Finger Paint 64
Cookie Cutter Stamps 65
Sponge Stamps 65
Raw Potato Stamps 65

Sidewalk Chalk Designs 66
Stencil Decorations.. 66
Paper Sack Gift Bags 66
Manila Envelope Gift Bags... 66
Gift Baskets 68
Gift Tags 68

7. **Gone but Never Forgotten:**
   Remembering Deceased Loved Ones.................................. 73
   Decorating the Grave of a Loved One 73
   Christmas Eve Graveside Candlelight Ceremony.................. 74
   Individual and Family Histories 74

8. **Preserving Memories**.. 75
   Creating a Christmas Memory Book 75
   Family Videos.. 76

9. **Tasty Treats**... 79
   Easy Chocolate and Caramel Pretzel Sticks 79
   Santa's Favorite Soft Sugar Cookies 80
   Christmas Eve Scones and Honey Butter............................ 81
   Award-winning Chocolate Chip Cookies 82
   Traditional Mint Brownies 82
   Delicious Fudge... 83
   Grandpa's Famous Oatmeal Cookies.................................. 84
   Caramel Popcorn.. 84
   Chocolate Marshmallow Bars 85
   Family Favorite Fruit Salad... 86
   Traditional Gingerbread House 86
   Easy Gingerbread House for Children................................ 88
   No-bake Shaggy Dawgs.. 91
   Homemade Root Beer 91
   Peppermint Bark.. 92
   Cookie Cutter Patterns... 93

10. **"Caroling, Caroling, Now We Go"**................................ 103
    A Collection of Traditional Christmas Carols 104
    Index of Christmas Carols... 124

11. Fun and Games 125
The Candy Cane Game (Spoons) 125
The Magic Elf Game 126
Snow Fun—The Fox and the Hound 127
Puzzles, Games, and Bingo 127
    Word Finds 128
    Christmas Match Game 131
    Crossword Puzzles 135
    Christmas Bingo 138
    Jigsaw Puzzles 158
    Answer Keys to Word Finds and Crossword Puzzles 160

12. Holiday Traditions 161

13. To Light His Way: The Beauty of Luminaries 164
Luminary Patterns 166

14. Enjoy the Magic of the Holidays: The Symbols of Christmas ... 170

15. "If Ye Have Done It unto The Least of These" Volunteerism and Service 173
Homeless Shelters and Soup Kitchens 173
Reputable Charities 174
Guess Who? Anonymously Make Someone's Christmas Brighter 174

16. The Reason We Celebrate Christmas: The Birth of Our Savior, Jesus Christ 175
The First Christmas: A Nativity Pageant for Children 176
Basic Nativity Costume 178
Nativity Costume Pattern 180

Acknowledgments

When I first started this project, I had no idea how much work it would be. I could not have done it without the help of a lot of wonderful people.

I want to express my appreciation to Grandma Rae, Laura H. White, Kathryn H. Clark, Elizabeth H. Stuart, and Kimberly Beth Stuart for their creative ideas; to Kevin and Ann Stuart for their color expertise; to Grandpa Doug, Laurie Hansen, Nicole Chamberlain, and Robert Haymond for their tasty recipes; to Annaliese Cox for testing recipes; to Mary Elizabeth Stuart for donning my nativity costume and allowing me to photograph her in it; to Heidi J. Doxey for catching my mistakes and for all her excellent suggestions; to Kammi Rencher and Kimiko Christensen Hammari for reviewing and endorsing my completed manuscript; and to Nicole Williams for the beautiful cover.

The projects, games, and activities in this book have been Holm family favorites for years, and I'm hoping to bring at least a little joy into the lives of others through my efforts. Thank you—all of you—for making it worthwhile!

Introduction

*C*hristmas is a season of miracles. It is a messenger of love, a reminder of good tidings, and a beacon of friendship and understanding. It can soften hearts, cleanse souls, and heal wounded spirits. Without the miracle of our Savior's birth and the sanctuary of the annual holiday season, the world would indeed be a lonely and hopeless place.

For me, discovering the magic of Christmas is to participate in holiday activities with my family. The following pages contain many of the things we have done together throughout the years. I hope you enjoy them as much as we have!

As you begin your projects, keep in mind that some of the patterns will need to be enlarged on a copy machine. If you do not have access to a copier, the patterns are also available on a CD-ROM. The CD-ROM contains a copy of this book and a pdf of each pattern in its original size. To order the CD-ROM, call Cedar Fort at 1-800-skybook, or visit their website at www.cedarfort.com.

Because of the beauty and enlightenment that the holiday season inspires, we sometimes forget that Christmas is also the busiest and most stressful time of year. We become so involved in planning and preparing that we run out of time to enjoy the results of our labors. A day is only twenty-four hours long, and we must learn to use those hours wisely. That doesn't mean we should jam everything into one day, one week, or even one month. A wise man once counseled that it is not requisite that a man should run faster than he has strength. Let us take his advice and not overdo this year.

May you have a peaceful and joyous holiday season!

Chapter One
Organize Yourself

Getting organized can help ease some of the stress of a busy holiday season. The following tasks are sometimes overlooked until it's too late. Once you have added your own reminders in the spaces provided at the end of this chapter, this list will ensure that no task is left undone and that all expectations will be met this year.

1. Take time to worship God
2. Spend quality time with family
3. Make time to serve others
4. Plan a holiday budget
5. Decorate home inside and out
6. Update Christmas card list
7. Create gift list
8. Purchase stamps, gift bags, wrapping paper, tape, and ribbon
9. Sign and mail Christmas cards
10. Plan Christmas parties
11. Plan holiday travel and visits
12. Arrange for time off from work
13. Make arrangements for a babysitter, if necessary
14. Purchase gifts
15. Wrap gifts
16. Mail Christmas packages
17. Plan holiday menus
18. Grocery shop for holiday menu items and baking items
19. Christmas baking

20. House cleaning
21. Participate in Christmas caroling, choirs, and plays
22. Plan Christmas wardrobe
23. Whenever possible, prepare holiday meals in advance
24. Don't forget the little things, such as preparing holiday favors; purchasing last-minute gifts; stocking up on treats, finger foods, and condiments; turning on the holiday lights; lighting the candles; lighting a fire in the fireplace; and any other seemingly small detail of importance.
25. Relax and enjoy the season!

26. _____

27. _____

28. _____

29. _____

30. _____

31. _____

32. _____

33. _____

34. _____

35. _____

36. _____

37. _____

38. _____

39. _____

40. _____

Chapter Two
It's Time to Decorate

*D*ecorating doesn't need to be expensive or difficult. The following ideas have been around for a long time, and children can even participate in making most of them.

Simple Cross-stitch Ornaments
Original designs by Laura H. White

Materials (in Christmas colors of your choice)
    Cross-stitch fabric
    Embroidery floss (2-ply)
    Sewing thread to match felt
    Sewing needle
    Felt
    Fabric paint
    Ribbon or yarn
    Quilt batting (or something similar)
    Scissors
    Sequins, beads, buttons, and other decorations of your choice

Cross-stitch fabric by Regency Mills, Inc., was used on the designs in the photos, but any brand will work. Purchase enough for as many ornaments as you plan on making. The embroidery floss was Coats and Clark.

Directions

You can use whatever colors you want, but the patterns have been marked for the following:

Black = b
Blue = bl
Brown = br
Gold = go
Gray = gr
Green = g
Orange = o
Pink = pk
Purple = p
Red = r
White = w
Yellow = y

Using the basic cross-stitch method (counting the squares out from the center point of the pattern), fill in the squares with the suggested colors or the colors of your choice. Make sure your crossover stitches are all going in the same direction. (See figure 1.)

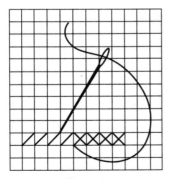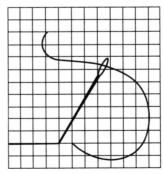

Figure 1   Figure 2

Some of the patterns indicate using an outline stitch, or the back stitch. (See figure 2.) You only need one strand of thread for this stitch. Bring your needle up through the first hole of the section that needs to be outlined. Place your needle down through the hole behind the initial stitch. This completes your first back stitch. Continue moving your needle and thread one stitch length back on top of the fabric and two stitch lengths forward beneath the fabric to form a solid line.

If desired, finish decorating your cross-stitch design by touching it up with fabric paint. There are several kinds available, including Scribbles Glittering Crystal, Tulip Glitter, and Tulip Slick by Duncan Enterprises.

When you've completed your cross-stitch design, mark it for cutting by using one of the frame patterns included in this chapter. The heavier broken line around the center opening on the pattern is the cutting line for the cross-stitch design, the lighter broken lines indicate where the seams should be made, and the solid center circle is the cutting line for the frame opening. (See photos and patterns on the following pages.)

Frame

Using one of the frame patterns provided (or a pattern of your choice), mark and cut your felt. Place the completed cross-stitch design in the round opening in the front piece of the frame. Baste it in place by hand. Hand baste a ribbon or yarn loop (for the ornament hanger) to the top back of the front piece.

Mark and cut your batting. (The batting should be cut at least ¼ inch smaller than the pattern you are using.) Place the batting between the front and back pieces and hand baste all three pieces in place. Following the pattern, stitch the front and back pieces together with a decorative stitch. Stitch around the center opening with a decorative stitch. Remove any excess batting that may be visible on the edges of the ornament.

Decorate with fabric paint, sequins, beads, buttons, ribbon, lace, or other embellishments. (See photos and cross-stitch patterns on the following pages.)

					gr	gr				
			gr	gr	gr		gr	gr		
		gr							gr	
					b	b		g	g	
				b	b	b	b	g	g	
			b	b	g	g	b	b	g	
		b	b	g	g	g	g	b	b	
	b	b	g	g	g	g	g	g	b	b
	b	g	g	g	g	g	g	g	g	b
		g	y	g	r	r	g	y	g	
		g	y	g	r	r	g	y	g	
		g	g	g	r	r	g	g	g	

House with heart frame

		y	y	y						
	y				y					
	y		go		y					
	y		go		y					
		r	r	r						
		r	r	r						
		r	r	r						
		r	r	r		g	g	g		
		r	r	r		g		g		
		r	r	r		g	g			
	g	g	g	g	g	g				
	g	g	g	g	g					

Candle with wreath frame

		g	g				g	g		
		g		g		g		g		
		g	g	g	g	g	g	g		
			g	r	r	r	g			
		g	r	r	r	r	g			
	g		r	r	r	r	r		g	
			r	r	r	r	r			
		go	go	go	go	go				
			r	r	r	r	r			
		r	r	r	r	r	r	r		
		r	r	r	r	r	r	r		
					go					

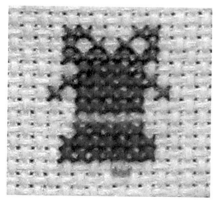

Bell

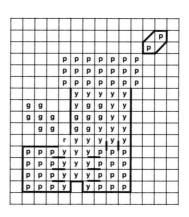

Stocking

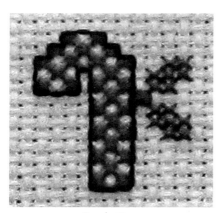

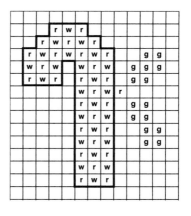

Candy Cane

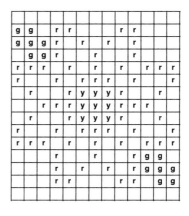

Poinsettia

7

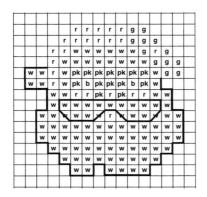

										p	p		
									p	pk	pk		
	p								p	pk	pk	pk	
p		p	pk	g	y	y	g	pk	pk		pk		
			pk	pk	g	g	g	g	pk	pk			
			pk	pk	pk	pk	pk	pk	pk	pk			
				pk	pk	pk	pk	pk	pk	pk			
				pk	pk					pk	pk		
			pk	pk						pk			
g			pk							pk			g
	g	pk								pk	g		
		g	g							g	g		
					g	g	g	g	g				

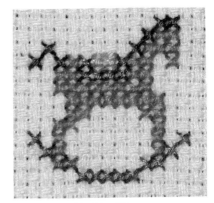

Rocking Horse

				r	r	r	r	r	g	g		
			r	r	r	r	r	r	g	g	g	
		r	r	w	w	w	w	w	w	g	r	g
	r	w	w	w	w	w	w	w	w	g	g	g
w	w	r	w	pk	pk	pk	pk	pk	pk	w	g	g
w	w	r	w	pk	b	pk	pk	pk	b	pk	w	
	w	w	r	r	pk	r	pk	r	r	w	w	
	w	w	w	w	w	w	w	w	w	w	w	
	w	w	w	w	r	w	r	w	w	w	w	w
	w	w	w	w	w	w	w	w	w	w	w	w
w	w	w	w	w	w	w	w	w	w	w	w	w
	w	w	w	w	w	w	w	w	w	w	w	
		w	w	w	w	w	w	w	w	w		
			w	w	w	w	w	w				

Santa

				y						
				g						
			g	g	g					
		g	g	r	g	g				
			g	g	g					
	g	p	g	g	bl	g	g			
		g	g	g	g	g				
g	g	g	r	g	g	g	o	g		
	g	g	g	g	g	g	g			
g	g	bl	g	g	g	p	g	g	g	g
				br						
				br						
				br						

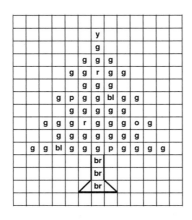

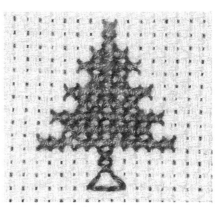

Christmas Tree

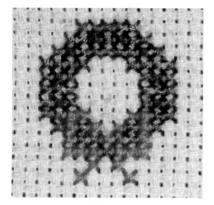

Wreath

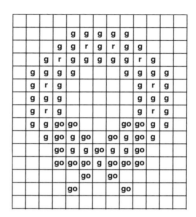

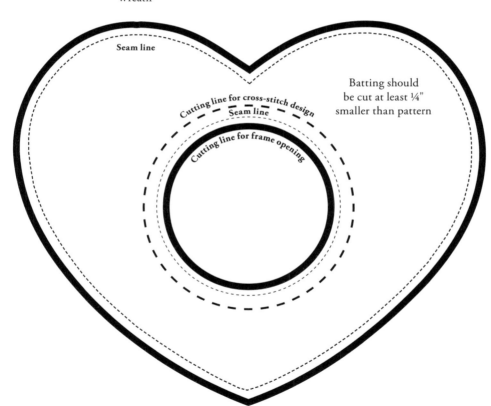

Seam line

Cutting line for cross-stitch design

Seam line

Cutting line for frame opening

Batting should
be cut at least ¼"
smaller than pattern

Heart frame for cross-stitch ornaments

Cut 2 (1 for the front with a round opening
and 1 for the back without an opening)
(See photo on page 6.)

9

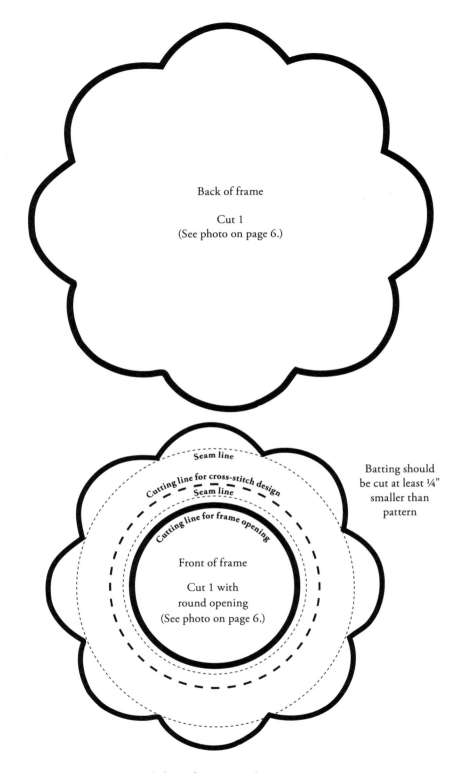

Back of frame

Cut 1
(See photo on page 6.)

Seam line

Cutting line for cross-stitch design

Seam line

Cutting line for frame opening

Front of frame

Cut 1 with
round opening
(See photo on page 6.)

Batting should
be cut at least ¼"
smaller than
pattern

Wreath frame for cross-stitch ornaments

Felt Christmas Tree Ornaments

Materials

Felt (in various Christmas colors of your choice)
Cookie cutter patterns on pages 93–102 (or your own patterns)
Scissors
Ribbon or yarn
Straight pins
Sewing thread (or yarn) to match felt
Tacky craft glue or glue gun
Quilt batting (or something similar)
Fabric paint
Sequins, beads, buttons, and other decorations of your choice

Directions

Fold the felt in half and pin the two halves together to hold them in place. Trace one of the cookie cutter patterns from pages 93–102 (or your own pattern) onto the felt. Following the traced pattern, cut through both layers so that you have two identical shapes.

Felt Christmas tree ornaments

Using the same pattern that was used for the felt, trace and cut one layer of batting for the stuffing. The batting must be cut at least ¼ inch smaller than the front and back pieces of the felt.

Hand baste or glue a ribbon (or yarn) loop to the top back of the front piece of the ornament.

Making sure that the basted or glued end of the ribbon will be inside the ornament, place the quilt batting between the two felt pieces. Sew or glue all three pieces together.

Decorate with fabric paint, sequins, beads, buttons, ribbon, lace, or other embellishments.

Old-fashioned Salt Dough Ornaments

Materials

Basic Salt Dough (see recipe below)
Cookie cutter patterns on pages 93–102
Water-based acrylic paint (in Christmas
colors of your choice)
Glitter (optional)
Paintbrushes
Craft wire
Wire cutters
Ornament hooks

Salt dough angel made with
a cookie cutter

Basic Salt Dough Recipe

3 cups flour
1½ cups salt
1½ cups water

Mix the salt and flour together. Gradually add the water. On a floured surface, knead until dough is stiff but pliable. If dough is too sticky, add more flour or salt.

Directions

Roll the dough out on a floured surface and use the cookie cutter patterns on pages 93–102 (or a pattern of your own) to cut shapes. For hanging the ornaments, push a loop of craft wire into the top back of each ornament. Place the ornaments on a cookie sheet and bake at 250 degrees for thirty minutes or until they have hardened.

When the ornaments have cooled, paint them with a water-based acrylic paint. A good brand is Apple Barrel, manufactured by Plaid Enterprises. If desired, add glitter to your designs before the paint dries.

Plaster of Paris Ornaments

Courtesy of Laura H. White

Materials

All-purpose plaster of paris
Candy molds in Christmas shapes
Water-based acrylic paint
Paintbrushes

Craft wire
Wire cutters
Glitter (optional)
Ornament hooks

Ornaments still in candy mold

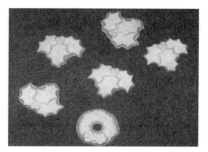

Unpainted ornaments

Handpainted horn

Handpainted Santa

Plaster of paris is inexpensive and is available at most craft stores. A popular brand is Kid's Kreations by Creative Crafts, Inc. A good candy mold is the Make 'n Mold's Candymaker, which is also available at most craft stores.

Handpainted sleigh

Directions

Mix the plaster according to the directions on the container. Pour the mixed plaster into Christmas candy molds. For hanging the ornaments, push a loop of craft wire into the top back of each ornament.

When your ornaments are dry, carefully remove them from the candy molds and paint them with a water-based acrylic paint. A good brand is Apple Barrel, manufactured by Plaid Enterprises. If desired, add glitter to your designs before the paint dries.

Beaded Ornaments

Chenille Pipe Cleaner and Bead Ornaments

These ornaments are especially fun for children to make.

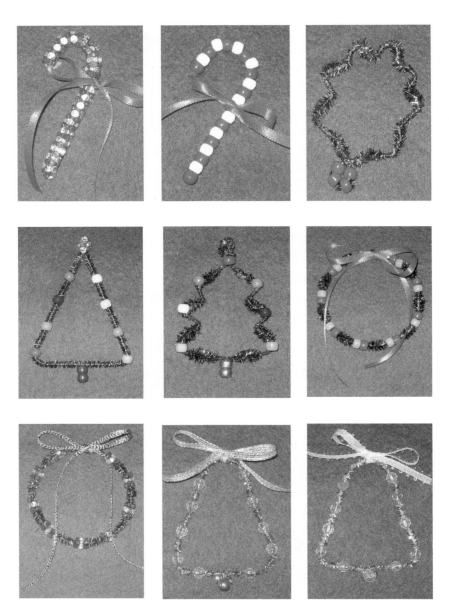

Materials

Chenille pipe cleaners   Various beads in Christmas colors   Ribbon

Chenille pipe cleaners can be purchased at your local craft store. There are several brands available, such as Chenille by Creative Hands and Sunburst Chenille Tinsel Bumps by Darcie. The Tinsel Bumps are especially fun to use because they are wider and fluffier. Pony beads and faceted beads by The Beadery work well for the wreaths, trees, and bells, but you may want to use Tri-beads by The Beadery (or another brand) for the candy canes. You can also use colored macaroni instead of beads (see page 25).

Directions

Shape your chenille pipe cleaner into a Christmas shape, such as a tree, a bell, or a wreath. With the exception of the candy canes, thread the beads ¾ inch apart on the pipe cleaner. For the candy canes, thread the beads close together. (See photos.) Twist the ends of the pipe cleaner together, and your ornament is complete.

Encourage your children to be creative. You'll be surprised at what they can do with a few beads and a pipe cleaner!

Crystal Icicle Ornament

Crystal Icicle Ornament

Courtesy of Kathryn H. Clark

Materials

1 (25 mm) crystal starflake bead
6 (18 mm) crystal starflake beads
4 (12 mm) crystal starflake beads
5 (10 mm) crystal facet beads
1 (8 mm) crystal facet bead
2 (6 mm) crystal facet beads
3 crystal spacer beads
Bead wire
Wire ribbon
Ornament hook
Needle-nose pliers or The Beadery's 3-in-1 Jewelry Maker's Tool

The beads in the photograph are Bits & Pieces by the Cousin Corporation. You can use any color you want to make your ornaments. The Jewelry Maker's Tool and the beads can be found at your local craft store.

Directions

With the needle-nose pliers, create a small loop on the end of the wire so the beads won't fall off. Add the following beads to the wire in this order: 1 (25 mm) starflake, 3 (18 mm) starflakes, 1 (10 mm) facet, 2 (18 mm) starflakes, 1 (10 mm) facet, 1 (18 mm) starflake, 1 (10 mm) facet, 2 (12 mm) starflakes, 1 (10 mm) facet, 2 (12 mm) starflakes, 1 (10 mm) facet, 1 (8 mm) facet, 2 (6 mm) facets, and 3 spacers.

Close off by making a small loop in the wire. Make sure it is closed enough so the beads won't fall off. Trim the wire. Add an ornament hook and a wire ribbon bow.

Crystal Loop Ornament

Courtesy of Kathryn H. Clark

Materials

Crystal Loop Ornament

    11 crystal spacer beads
    11 (6 mm) crystal facet beads
    4 (12 mm) crystal starflake beads
    2 (18 mm) crystal starflake beads
    1 (25 mm) crystal starflake bead
    Bead wire
    Wire ribbon
    Ornament hook
    Needle-nose pliers or The Beadery's 3-in-1 Jewelry Maker's Tool

The beads in the photograph are Bits & Pieces by the Cousin Corporation. You can use any color you want to make your ornaments. The Jewelry Maker's Tool and the beads can be found at your local craft store.

Directions

With the needle-nose pliers, create a small loop on the end of the wire so the beads won't fall off. Add the following beads to the wire in this order: 3 spacers, 1 (6 mm) facet, 1 spacer, 1 (6 mm) facet, 1 (12 mm) starflake, 1 (6 mm) facet, 1 (12 mm) starflake, 1 (6 mm) facet, 1 (18 mm) starflake, 1 (6 mm) facet, 1 (18 mm) starflake, 1 (25 mm) starflake, 1 (18 mm) starflake, 1 (6 mm) facet, 1 (18 mm) starflake, 1 (6 mm) facet, 1 (12 mm) starflake, 1 (6 mm) facet, 1 (12 mm) starflake, 1 (6 mm) facet, 1 spacer, 1 (6 mm) facet, 3 spacers. Thread the wire through the loop in the first end of the wire, but do not trim it yet. Pulling the wire tight, add 3 spacers and 1 (6 mm) facet and leave them to hang in the middle of the ornament. (See photo on page 15.) Close off by making a small loop. Trim the wire. Add an ornament hook and a wire ribbon bow.

Bead and Sequin Styrofoam Ball Ornaments

Courtesy of Elizabeth H. Stuart

Materials

1 (2" or 2½") Styrofoam ball

Sequins

Beads and decorations of your
choice that can be attached
with appliqué pins

Ribbon or decorative cording

Hat pins (optional)

Glue gun and glue sticks

Appliqué pins, size 12 (19 mm
or ¾")

Directions

This craft has been around for many years, and the finished product is surprisingly beautiful. Some of the ornaments in the photo were purchased in a kit, and some were not. I haven't been able to find kits for this project for the last several years, but even though the kits may not be available anymore, you can still easily design your own patterns.

Bead and sequin Styrofoam
ball ornaments

To create this ornament, use the appliqué pins (or hat pins if desired) to attach the sequins, beads, and ribbon to the Styrofoam ball. The finished product will be nicer if you can find pins with decorative heads, but that isn't absolutely necessary. Before you begin, draw a circle (representing the Styrofoam ball) on a piece of scratch paper and plan your design. If you are one of those talented people who do not have to plan ahead, you can create your design as you go. You can also use the ornaments in the photo as an example.

Glue a row of ribbon or decorative cording around the ball, leaving enough ribbon or cording at the top of the ball to tie a loop or a bow. Begin pinning the sequins, beads, or other decorations to the ball in the desired pattern. Continue doing this until the entire ball is covered. (See photo.)

To hang the ornament, tie a loop or a bow with the extra ribbon or cording at the top of the ball. Hang your ornament on your Christmas tree, fireplace, or wall and enjoy the compliments!

Faux Stained Glass Ornaments and Decorations

This is one of my favorites! I was surprised at how pretty they are. I made them in school when I was a child, but I don't remember them being so beautiful.

Materials

Permanent markers in multiple
    colors
Aluminum foil
Tacky craft glue
Cardboard or thick paper
Patterns (on the following pages)
Ornament hook (optional)

Faux stained glass decoration

The best brand of glue to use is Aleene's Original Tacky Glue. Sharpie fine-tip markers are the most versatile, because the same pen can get into both the wide areas and the tiny spaces around the glue.

Directions

Attach one of the stained glass patterns (or a pattern of your choice) to a piece of cardboard or heavy paper. You can cut the pattern out if it's an ornament shape, or leave it as a full page.

Thinly trace the dark lines on the pattern with tacky glue. Let the glue dry overnight or until it is completely solid.

When the glue is dry, cover the front and back of the pattern and the cardboard with aluminum foil, shiny side up. Using your fingers, gently smooth the foil over the glue lines so they stand out.

Color the sections of the stained glass ornament or window with permanent markers, but avoid coloring the glue lines. (See photo.) Punch a hole in the top of your design and add an ornament hook and a bow.

Faux stained glass ornament

Faux stained glass window

Faux stained glass star ornament

Advent Calendar

This calendar is perfect for children. It is colorful and bright and easy to make. You can find most of the materials at your local fabric or craft store.

Materials

Felt—2 (12" x 19") sheets each of 5 different bright Christmas colors
24" x 30" solid color heavy fabric (preferably green or red)
Wooden dowel—½" diameter by 32" long (If a longer dowel is the only size available, then cut the longer dowel down to size.)
60" of Christmas ribbon
Tacky craft glue
Number and alphabet patterns on pages 99–102
Pocket pattern on page 24
Wreath and bow patterns on page 25
Decorative-edged scissors
Candy or small ornaments to place in the pockets of the calendar (Reduced in size, the felt Christmas tree ornaments on page 11 will work perfectly.)
22" x 28" poster board (optional) (It's harder to store the calendar if it is attached to a poster board.)
Fabric paint (optional)
Glitter glue (optional)
Other decorations, such as sequins, beads, gems, or bows (optional)

Directions

Pockets

Using decorative-edged scissors, cut 5 (3½- by 3-inch) squares from each color of felt. (See pattern on page 24.) When you have finished cutting the felt, you should have 25 squares (or pockets).

Calendar

Sew a 1-inch hem on the sides and bottom edges of the heavy fabric. Hem the top edge last, leaving enough space in the hem to insert the dowel.

If heavy fabric is not available, do not hem the fabric. Attach it to a poster board instead, by gluing the sides and bottom edges of the fabric to the back of the board. Don't glue the fabric to the front of the board, except for the top edge. You will want to insert the dowel there, so you will need to glue the fabric along the top edge of the poster board and fold the fabric over the dowel. Once the dowel is in place, glue the fabric to the back of the board. Be sure to allow enough time for the glue to dry. You can also leave the dowel off and attach the calendar to the wall with thumbtacks.

Advent calendar

Letters and Numbers

Once you've decided on a title for your calendar, enlarge and cut out the alphabet patterns on pages 99–102 and trace them onto the five different colors of felt. The idea is to make your calendar colorful, so use all the colors. Don't use foam on the title or pocket numbers unless you have purchased ready-made foam letters and numbers, or if you have a personal shape cutter. Foam is thick and hard to cut, and since the letters are small, they will be even more difficult to cut.

Cut the letters out and glue them to the top of the calendar. Arrange them on the calendar before you glue them so you can make sure they are straight, evenly spaced, and properly centered.

Enlarge, cut out, and trace onto the felt the number patterns on pages 101–2. You will need numbers 1–24. Carefully glue them onto the pockets. Decorate

Christmas Day pocket

23

the numbers and pockets with fabric paint, glitter glue, beads, sequins, or other embellishments. Children love to do this, so get them involved.

For the Christmas Day pocket, use the wreath and bow patterns on the following page. Or you can use any of the patterns on pages 93–102 or a pattern of your own choosing. You can also place the number 25 on the Christmas Day pocket instead of a Christmas shape.

Place the pockets on the calendar and line them up correctly before you glue them on. If you place them 1 inch from the edges of the calendar fabric, you can space them evenly all the way up to the title. Placing the pockets is one of the most difficult parts of making the calendar, so be patient and careful. It may not be perfect, but it will look nice even if it isn't exact.

Attach the ribbon to the dowel and place your calendar so that your children can easily reach it. Beginning on December 1, remove the ornament from the first pocket and hang it on your tree. Or have your children take turns removing and eating the candy from the appropriate pocket each day.

Advent calendar pocket, 3½" x 3"
Cut 25

Bow and wreath
for Christmas Day
advent calendar pocket

Garlands

Bead Garland

Buy inexpensive pony beads and string them on fishing line, heavy thread, or yarn. Use them as garland on your tree. It can be beautiful!

Macaroni Garland

As simple and outdated as it may seem, children still enjoy stringing colored macaroni for tree garland. Macaroni can also be used instead of beads for the chenille pipe cleaner ornaments on page 14.

Materials
4 cups macaroni
½ cup white (or clear) vinegar mixed with 2 cups water
Food coloring (enough to make a bright color)
Newspaper
Paper towel

Directions

Mix the vinegar, water, and food coloring together. Add the macaroni and stir well until it has absorbed enough color. (Be careful not to leave it in the water too long.) Place newspaper and then paper towels on your table or countertop. Spread the macaroni on the paper towels and leave it there until it dries. String the macaroni on fishing line (or strong thread or yarn) and add the garland to your Christmas tree.

Popcorn Garland

Pop approximately five bags (or less, depending on how much garland you want to make) of salt-free, butterless microwave popcorn. String the popcorn with a needle on fine fishing line (or sewing thread). Once you have strung the popcorn, you can color it by spraying it lightly with spray paint. (Caution: If you spray paint the popcorn, make sure your children understand that it is no longer edible.)

Homemade Candles

Keep in mind that wax is flammable and can ignite at approximately 400 degrees. Adult supervision of children is necessary when making candles.

Materials

Homemade candles

Paraffin wax for as many candles as you intend to make (This depends on the size of your molds.)

Tapered candles (or string) for wicks

Crayons for color (optional)

Double boiler pan

A clean can

Crushed ice (optional)

Wooden stick or spoon

Containers of various sizes and shapes (preferably discarded milk or cottage cheese cartons, especially those coated with wax; or you can use glass containers)

Wooden stick or ruler

Directions

Put at least 2 inches of water in the bottom of the double boiler. Break or cut the paraffin wax into small pieces and place the pieces in a clean can. (You can also use the top of the double boiler if you want to take the time afterward to clean out the wax.) Put the can directly into the water in the bottom of the double boiler. For safety reasons, warm on low heat.

If you want a colored candle, cut a colored crayon into pieces and add it to the melted wax. Stir well for an even color.

Cut the tapered candle on the bottom (wide) end so that it is the same height as the mold. Anchor the taper by pouring at least ½ inch of melted wax into the bottom of the mold. Hold the taper in place a few minutes until the wax has set. If you are not using ice, fill the mold to the top with melted wax.

If you want to use string for the wick, you must attach a weight to the string to anchor it in place when you add the hot wax. To do this, tie a small decorative rock (or a clean rock from outside) to one end of the string and center the rock in the bottom of the mold.

Using masking tape, secure a stick or a wooden ruler across the top of the mold. Tie the other end of the string to the ruler. Make sure the rock and the string are centered properly before you add the melted wax. If using ice, at this point you should only add 1 inch of melted wax to the bottom of the mold to hold the rock in place. If you are not using ice, fill the mold to the top with melted wax.

If you want your candle to have a lacy appearance, you can add crushed ice to the melted wax. (Note: This will not work with glass molds because the water from the melted ice won't be able to drain from the hardened candle.) Here's how:

Once your taper (or wick) is anchored into the wax, carefully place a layer of crushed ice (or small ice cubes, depending on the desired appearance) around the taper. Add melted wax until the ice is almost completely covered. Add more ice and more wax, more ice and more wax, alternating between the two until the mold is full. You may want to experiment by remelting the wax until the desired appearance is achieved.

Because the mold will leak water as the wax cools, you will need to place it in a bowl or a pan and let it sit until the wax has hardened completely. Remove the mold by carefully tearing or peeling it off the candle. You can add decorations such as glitter, beads, or sequins to your candle, but you can't light it if you do this.

Tissue Paper Christmas Wreath

Materials

Wire hanger (or other pliable wire)

Approximately 16 sheets (2 pkgs.) of colorful 20" x 26" Christmas tissue paper, double sided, if possible (You can use tissue paper as small as 20" x 20", but it will be harder to tie the paper onto the hanger.)

Tissue paper wreath

Small Christmas tree ornaments (optional)
Glue gun and glue sticks (optional)
Bow
Wire cutters

Directions

Using pliers or your hands, bend the wire hanger into a circle. Leave the hook on if you want to use it to hang your wreath. Otherwise, cut it off with the wire cutters.

Cut the tissue paper into 5- by 13-inch lengths (5- by 10-inch lengths if using 20" x 20" paper). One at a time, tie the pieces onto the wire hanger and push them together as close as possible. If you are working with one-sided tissue, make sure you tie it onto the wire with the printed side up.

Continue to tie the paper on the hanger until the hanger is completely covered. When you have finished making your wreath, trim it so that it is even all the way around.

If your wreath is a solid color, you may want to add some contrasting colors. Small Christmas tree ornaments will work perfectly. Carefully glue them onto the wreath. Add a bow and proudly display your masterpiece where everyone can see it. If you wish, you can make garland in the same way by using heavy string or fishing line instead of a wire hanger.

Snow Globes

Materials

Jar with watertight lid
Glue gun and glue sticks
Small bottle cap (optional)
Plastic Christmas figurine
Crystal Glitter by Glitterex Corp.
Silver Glitter (optional)
Mouth wash (comparable to Equate
    Antiseptic Mouth Rinse)
Ribbon or lace (optional)
Spray paint (optional)

Snow Globes

Directions

Avoid using a decorative jar, because you won't be able to see the figurine through the glass.

The best glitter to use is the white Crystal Glitter by Glitterex Corp. It looks more like sparkling snow and stays suspended in the water for a longer period of time.

Leaving enough space to screw the lid onto the jar, glue a small bottle cap (top side up) to the inside of the jar lid. Glue the Christmas figurine to the top of the bottle cap. (This allows the Christmas figurine to be viewed above the lid of the jar.) Allow enough time for the glue to dry.

When the glue is dry, fill the jar almost to the top with lukewarm water. Add 1 tablespoon mouth wash and ¾ teaspoon crystal glitter for every ½ pint (1 cup) water. The mouth wash helps the glitter stay suspended in the water for a longer period of time. It also prevents it from clumping. Variation: Add ¾ teaspoon crystal glitter and a sprinkle of silver glitter for every ½ pint (1 cup) of water.

Tightly secure the lid on the jar so it won't leak. Shake the jar well. Let it sit overnight to allow the glitter to become saturated. Don't decorate the glass or you won't be able to see the figurine; however, you can decorate the lid by gluing ribbon or lace around it or by spray painting it.

Mini Christmas Stockings

Materials

Felt (in various Christmas colors of
    your choice)
Mini Christmas stocking patterns
    on the following page
Sewing thread to match felt
Glue gun or tacky craft glue
Fabric paint
Sequins, beads, buttons, and other
    decorations of your choice
Scissors

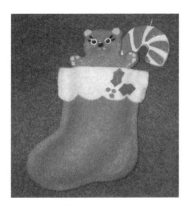

Mini Christmas stocking
with salt dough ornaments

Directions

Using the patterns provided, mark and cut your felt. You will need two pieces—one for the front of the stocking and one for the back.

Leaving an opening at the top of the stocking, stitch or glue the front and back pieces together. Glue the trim around the top of the stocking. (See photo.) Decorate with fabric paint, sequins, beads, buttons, ribbon, lace, or other decorations. Fill the stocking with goodies or other small surprises.

Stocking trim

Mini Christmas stocking

Chapter Three
Once upon a Time

What is the holiday season without a Christmas story or two? Everyone has seen *How the Grinch Stole Christmas*, *Frosty the Snowman*, *Rudolph the Red-Nosed Reindeer*, and *The Night Before Christmas*. They are all classics, and some are even considered traditions.

Suggested Movies

The following movies are not only entertaining, but they are also appropriate for the whole family. This is only a partial list of movies that can be considered safe for both young and old audiences. Not all of them are Christmas related, so you may want to watch some of them even after the holidays.

All That Heaven Allows
Amadeus
An Affair to Remember
Andre Rieu—The Christmas I Love
Babes in Toyland
Back to the Future movies
Beauty and the Beast, Enchanted Christmas
Bedknobs and Broomsticks
Best Years of Our Lives, The
Bishop's Wife, The
Blackbeard's Ghost
Bridge to Terabithia

Caroline
Casper
Cat Ballou
Charlie Brown Christmas, A
Cheaper by the Dozen
Christmas Box
Christmas Carol, A
Christmas on Sesame Street
Christmas Shoes, The
Christmas Story
Christmas with Andre Rieu
Citizen Kane
Dial "M" for Murder
Egg and I, The
Enchanted
Fallen Angel
Farewell to Arms, A
Fiddler on the Roof
Four Feathers, The
Frosty the Snowman
Galaxy Quest
Gaslight
Ghost and Mr. Chicken, The
Ghost and Mrs. Muir, The
Gift of Love, The
Good-bye, Mr. Jordan
Greatest Story Ever Told, The
Grinch, The
Harry Potter movies
Hearts in Atlantis
Heaven Can Wait
Heiress, The
Holes
Home Improvement TV series
Hometown Christmas
How the Grinch Stole Christmas
Indiana Jones movies
It Happened One Christmas

It's a Wonderful Life
Jane Eyre
Keeper of the Flame
King and I, The
Laura
Letter to Three Wives
Little Lord Fauntleroy
Little Princess, The
Little Women
Love Comes Softly
Magic of Ordinary Days, The
Magnificent Obsession
Make Mine Mink
Maltese Falcon, The
Mary Christmas
Mary Poppins
Mickey's Christmas Carol
Midnight Hour
Miracle on 34th Street
Mr. Magoo's Christmas Carol
Mrs. Miniver
Mummy, The, movies
Muppet Christmas Carol
Muppet Family Christmas, A
Muppet Christmas Movie
My Fair Lady
Narnia movies
Night Before Christmas, The
Nightmare Before Christmas, The
Nutcracker, The
O. Henry's Full House
Only You
Our Mutual Friend
Parent Trap
Paint Your Wagon
Persuasion
Phone Call from a Stranger
Pirates of the Caribbean movies

Polar Express, The
Pollyanna
Portrait of Dorian Gray, The
Portrait of Jenny
Pride and Prejudice
Princess Bride, The
Random Harvest
Rear Window
Rebecca
Remember the Titans
Return to Me
Rigoletto
Rudolph the Red-Nosed Reindeer
Santa Claus, The, movies
Savannah Smiles
Scarlet Pimpernel, The
Secondhand Lions
Secret Garden, The
Sense and Sensibility
Shadowlands
Shane
Shop Around the Corner, The
Shrek movies
Signs
Snow White and the Three Stooges
Song of Bernadette, The
Sound of Music, The
Stardust
Steel Magnolias
Support Your Local Sheriff
Swan Princess, The
Ten Commandments, The
Tender Mercies
Then There Were None
Three Lives of Thomasina, The
Thumbelina
To Kill a Mockingbird
Toy Story movies

Troll in Central Park, The
Tuck Everlasting
Uninvited, The
Vertigo
Village, The
Walk to Remember, A
Walt Disney Christmas, A
When Angels Come to Town
White Christmas
Wide Awake
Wiggley Christmas
Willy Wonka and the Chocolate Factory
Winnie the Pooh: A Very Merry Pooh Year
Winnie the Pooh: Seasons of Giving
Wizard of Oz, The
Wuthering Heights

Suggested Books and Short Stories

Again, some of these classics are not Christmas related, but they are all worth reading. You will find these, and many other wonderful tales, in your public library. Happy reading!

Adventures of Huckleberry Finn, The, Mark Twain
Adventures of Tom Sawyer, The, Mark Twain
Aesop's Fables, William Caxton (Translation)
Alice's Adventures in Wonderland, Lewis Carroll
Anne Frank, Diary of a Young Girl
Anne of Green Gables, Lucy Maud Montgomery
Beauty, Robin McKinley
Bipper and Wick, Artie Knapp
Black Beauty, Anna Sewell
Blue Bird, The, Madame d'Aulnoy
Call of the Wild, Jack London
Christmas at Fezziwig's Warehouse, Charles Dickens
Christmas Box, The, Richard Paul Evans
Christmas Carol, A, Charles Dickens
Christmas Cuckoo, The, Frances Browne
Christmas Fairy, A, John Strange Winter

Christmas Fairy of Strasburg (German Folktale), J. Stirling Coyne

Christmas in the Alley, Olive Thorne Miller

Christmas in the Barn, F. Arnstein

Christmas Masquerade, The, Mary E. Wilkins Freeman

Christmas Star, A, Katherine Pyle

Christmas Thorn of Glastonbury: A Legend of Ancient Britain, William of Malmesbury

Christmas Under the Snow, Olive Thorne Miller

Cinderella, Strabo (Greek)

Clever Little Tailor, Brothers Grimm

Cratchits' Christmas Dinner, The, Charles Dickens

C. S. Lewis's books

David Copperfield, Charles Dickens

Elves and the Shoemaker, The, Brothers Grimm

Emperor's New Clothes, The, Hans Christian Andersen

First New England Christmas, The, G. L. Stone and M.G. Fickett

Frog Prince, The, Brothers Grimm

Gift of the Magi, The, O. Henry

Golden Slipper, The, Alexander Afanasyev

Good Stories for Great Holidays, Frances Olcott Jenkins

Greatest of These, The, Joseph Mills Hanson

Grimm's Fairy Tales, Jacob and Wilhelm Grimm

Gulliver's Travels, Jonathan Swift

Hans Brinker and the Silver Skates, Mary Mapes Dodge

Hans Christian Andersen Fairy Tales

Happy Prince and Other Tales, The, Oscar Wilde

Harry Potter books, J. K. Rowling

Heidi, Johanna Spyri

How the Grinch Stole Christmas, Dr. Seuss

Ivanhoe, Walter Scott

Jack and the Beanstalk, Joseph Jacobs

Jane Eyre, Charlotte Brontë

Jimmy Scarecrow's Christmas, Mary E. Wilkins Freeman

Journey to the Centre of the Earth, Jules Verne

Jungle Book, Rudyard Kipling

Kidnapped Santa Claus, A, L. Frank Baum

Kidnapped, Robert Louis Stevenson

King Arthur and His Knights, Howard Pyle
King Solomon's Mines, H. Rider Haggard
Legend of Sleepy Hollow The, Washington Irving
Life and Adventures of Santa Claus, The, L. Frank Baum
Life of Our Lord, The, Charles Dickens
Little Girl's Christmas, Winnifred E. Lincoln
Little Gretchen and the Wooden Shoe, Elizabeth Harrison
Little House on the Prairie, Laura Ingalls Wilder
Little Lord Fauntleroy, Frances Hodgson Burnett
Little Match Girl, The, Hans Christian Andersen
Little Mermaid, The, Hans Christian Andersen
Little Princess, A, Frances Hodgson Burnett
Little Women, Louisa May Alcott
Lost World, The, Arthur Conan Doyle
Master Sandy's Snapdragon, Elbridge S. Brooks
Merry Adventures of Robin Hood, Howard Pyle
Night Before Christmas, The, Clement Clarke Moore
Old Father Christmas, J. H. Ewing
Persuasion, Jane Austen
Peter Pan, J. M. Barrie
Philanthropist's Christmas, The, James Weber Linn
Pilgrim's Progress, John Bunyan
Pine Tree, The, Hans Christian Andersen
Pinocchio, Carlo Collodi
Pollyanna, Eleanor H. Porter
Pride and Prejudice, Jane Austen
Prince and the Pauper, The, Mark Twain
Princess and the Goblin, The, George MacDonald
Puss in Boots, Charles Perrault
Queerest Christmas, The, Grace Margaret Gallaher
Railway Children, The, E. Nesbit
Rapunzel, The Brothers Grimm
Rebecca of Sunnybrook Farm, Kate Douglas Wiggin
Rebecca, Daphne Du Maurier
Red Shoes, The, Hans Christian Andersen
Rip Van Winkle, Washington Irving
Robinson Crusoe, Daniel Defoe

Rumpelstiltskin, Brothers Grimm

Saint Nicholas Tale: The Baker's Dozen, A, Aaron Shepard

Screwtape Letters, The, C. S. Lewis

Secret Garden, The, Frances Hodgson Burnett

Seven Ravens, The, Brothers Grimm

Seven Stories of Christmas Love, Leo Buscaglia

Shadowlands, Leonore Fleischer

Six Swans, The, Brothers Grimm

Sleeping Beauty, Charles Perrault

Snow White, Brothers Grimm

Stories of Faith for Christmas, Guideposts

Swiss Family Robinson, Johann Rudolf Wyss

Tales of Mother Goose, Charles Perrault

Tales of Peter Rabbit, Beatrix Potter

Three Billy Goats Gruff, Peter Chr. Asbjørnsen and Jørgen Moe

Three Kings of Cologne: A Legend of the Middle Ages,
     John of Hildesheim

Three Little Pigs, Joseph Jacobs

Three Musketeers, The, Alexandre Dumas, père

Through the Looking Glass, Lewis Carroll

Thumbelina, Hans Christian Andersen

Timeless Wisdom—The Best of Dr. Frank Crane's Four-Minute Essays,
     Compiled by K. R. Talbot

Tinder Box, The, Hans Christian Andersen

To Kill a Mockingbird, Harper Lee

Toinette and the Elves, Susan Coolidge

Treasure Island, Robert Louis Stevenson

Tuck Everlasting, Natalie Babbitt

Twelve Dancing Princesses, The, Brothers Grimm

Twenty Thousand Leagues under the Sea, Jules Verne

Ugly Duckling, The, Hans Christian Andersen

Voyage of the Wee Red Cap, The, Ruth Sawyer Durand

Where the Red Fern Grows, Wilson Rawls

Why Evergreens Never Lose Their Leaves, Florence Holbrook

Why the Chimes Rang, Raymond McAlden

Wind in the Willows, The, Kenneth Grahame

Wonderful Wizard of Oz, The, L. Frank Baum

World's Best Fairy Tales, The, Volumes I and II, Reader's Digest

Chapter Four
Greetings to a Friend

Greeting cards can be simple or extravagant depending on how much time you want to spend on them.

Some people prefer the layered scrapbook style, while others prefer the old-fashioned kind with lots of glitter. Embossing can be time consuming, but the finished product is always worth the effort. In the end, what really counts is the spirit in which the card was created, and anything goes nowadays. A handmade greeting is fashioned with love, and the recipient is almost always honored to receive it.

Here are a few ideas that may come in handy when you are considering your Christmas cards.

Embossing

Embossing is nothing more than ornamenting your card with a pattern that stands out from (or is raised above) the rest of the paper.

The tools for this art can be extremely expensive, and the art itself can be time consuming. If you are living on a small budget, or if you don't have a lot of time, you may want to avoid this craft.

To begin, you will need a good light table. The best one for the money is the Fiskars® Shape Boss, which costs twenty to thirty dollars. It is 8½ by 11 inches and comes with a starter set of one stylus and one stencil. It also comes with embossing instructions. You can use this light table to trace patterns or other items, so it's well worth the money. The Shape Boss is available at your local craft store.

A less expensive light table is the Embossing Essentials Light Table by

Darice. At 6 by 9 inches, it is much smaller than the Shape Boss and does not come with a starter set. It costs anywhere from nine to sixteen dollars.

The embossing stylus is relatively inexpensive and can be found at most craft stores. I prefer the Dual-Tip Stylus Detail Burnishers by Fiskars®. You get more for your money, and the Dual-Tips usually sell for less than three dollars. They are convenient because they come in different sizes.

Embossing punches can save you time and give you the same beautiful appearance that a stylus does, but the punches cost anywhere from twelve to twenty dollars each and usually come with only one pattern.

You can make your own embossing stencils or purchase a commercial brand. If you decide to use your own pattern, you will need to at least look at a commercial stencil so you will know how to make one. Fiskars® seems to have the least expensive stencils on the market, and they cost anywhere from two to twelve dollars. You get more for your money by purchasing these, because they usually have several sheets with several designs in each package.

If you want to create your own stencil, you must make two identical stencils instead of one. The first one goes under your card to raise it up so you can use the holes in it to make indentations in your card. The second one is placed on top of your card for a pattern. The patterns on the two stencils must be lined up exactly for them to work properly.

To emboss, you press indentations into the paper by using the stylus and by following the patterns in the top stencil. A light table is necessary so you can see the bottom stencil patterns through your paper; otherwise, you won't be able to make the indentations in your card.

Embossing sounds complicated, but it's really quite simple. More detailed instructions should be included with your light table when you purchase it.

Glitter

If you are going to use glitter on a greeting card, then you need to use the right kind. The best brand is Sparkles Diamond Paper Glitter by PSX Design, but it's sometimes difficult to find. That's why I'm recommending Crystal or Icicle Stickles by Ranger. The bottles only contain .5 fluid ounces of glitter glue, but one bottle goes a long way.

Keep the glitter light and use your best judgment on where to place it. If you keep it simple, then your card can't help but turn out perfect.

Scrapbooking Cards

These cards are extremely popular nowadays, and you can get away with doing just about anything. I've seen cards that were made out of wrapping paper, paper sacks, or old newspapers. I've seen them decorated with buttons, ribbon, yarn, felt, safety pins, rivets, commercial baubles, and candy. You can purchase ready-made shapes and clip art, some of which are reasonably priced. These include Creative Hands Smart Foam and Colorbok Deluxe Chipboard in a Bucket. To give you some ideas, I've included a few photos of cards I've either made or received in the last few years, and pages 42–46 include additional ideas and clip art for greeting cards. Have fun!

Scrapbooking cards, printed cards with glitter, and an embossed card

For unto us a child is born

Unto us a son is given:
and the government shall
be upon his shoulders; and
his name shall be called
Wonderful, Counsellor,
The mighty God,
The everlasting Father,
The Prince of Peace.

~ Isaiah 9:6

From our
home to
yours!

Greetings for the inside of the cards

Clip art for
greeting cards

Greeting Card Holder

Our family made one of these when I was a child, and my mother still uses it after more than thirty years. (See photo.) The only thing she has replaced through the years is the plastic plate and the top decoration.

Materials

A plastic plate, preferably red or green (The plate can also be Styrofoam, metal, or paper.)

An empty wrapping paper cylinder (or something similar; the larger in diameter the better)

Yarn, preferably red or green

A bow, silk poinsettia, or something else that will completely cover the top of the cylinder

Glue gun

Large canning jar lid (optional)

Card holder

Directions

Glue the first end of the yarn inside the cylinder.

Vertically wrap the cylinder with even strands of yarn. (See photo.) Once the cylinder is completely covered, glue the tail end of the yarn inside the cylinder. For storage purposes, it is best to glue a large canning jar lid (or something else that is attractive and will still fit) to the bottom end of the cylinder for a base. If a canning jar lid is not available, glue the bottom end of the cylinder directly to the plate. If you plan on using the holder for more than one year, keep in mind that it will be harder to store with the plate glued to the bottom.

Card holder with cards

Top the cylinder with a bow, a silk poinsettia, or something else that will completely cover the hole in the top of the cylinder.

To display your cards, carefully slip them through the strands of yarn. (See photo.) This is especially nice because you can read your cards without removing them from the holder.

Chapter Five
Simple Gift Ideas

The following gift suggestions may not be as fancy as some of the things you can buy in a store, but they will definitely touch the hearts of those who receive them!

Homemade Gift Boxes

These boxes filled with goodies or small trinkets are perfect for a special friend or neighbor. (See patterns on the following pages.) Children especially enjoy making and decorating them, and it's a nice way to get your children involved in the family's Christmas preparations.

I've included the patterns for two boxes. Use card stock when you print or copy them so they will be more solid. Fold the markings and instructions inside the box, or trace the pattern on a clean sheet of paper so the markings and instructions won't show on the outside. You can use a glue stick or invisible tape to attach the sides and bottoms of the box.

The dotted lines on the patterns identify areas of the box that need to be folded. The solid lines are areas that need to be cut.

On the first gift box, the numbers identify the order in which the flaps must be folded and inserted into the bottom of the box to form the bottom of the box.

Once your box has been constructed, decorate it with stickers, glitter, beads, sequins, ribbons, bows, and glass gems from your local craft store. Be sure to assembly the box before you decorate it; otherwise, you may lose some of the decorations when you try to fold it.

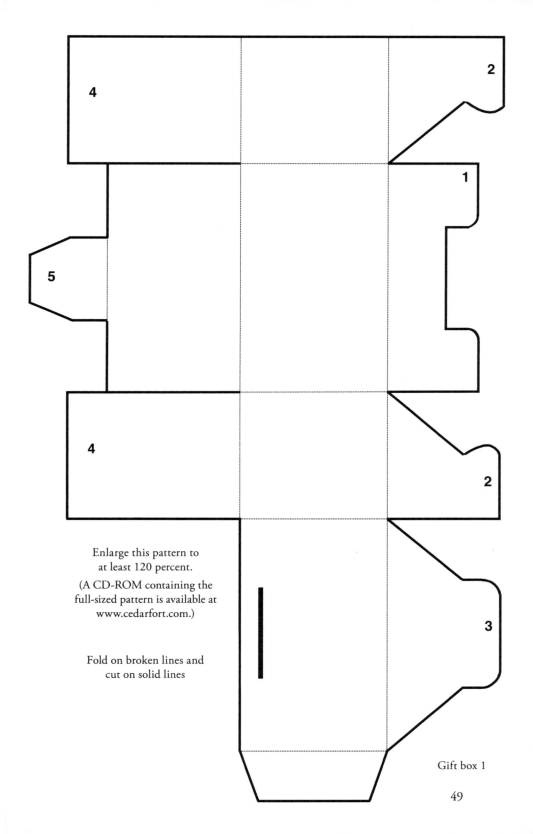

4

2

1

5

4

2

Enlarge this pattern to
at least 120 percent.

(A CD-ROM containing the
full-sized pattern is available at
www.cedarfort.com.)

Fold on broken lines and
cut on solid lines

3

Gift box 1

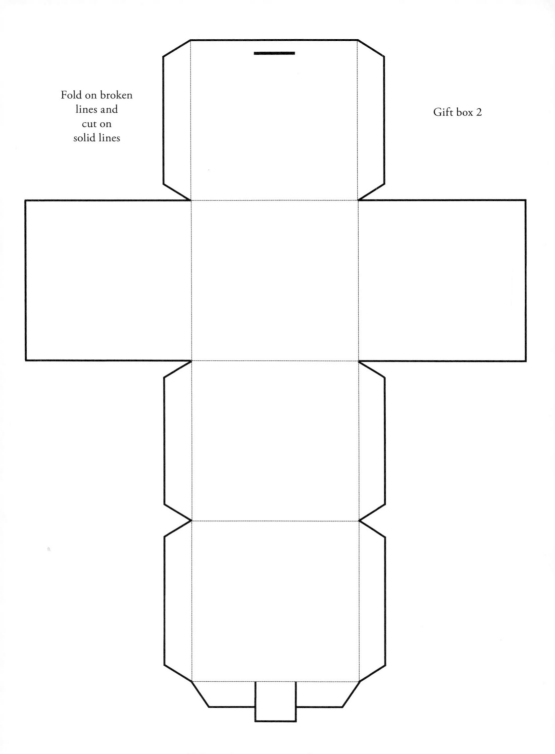

Fold on broken
lines and
cut on
solid lines

Gift box 2

Enlarge this pattern to at least 130 percent.
(A CD-ROM containing the full-sized pattern is available at www.cedarfort.com.)

Gift Baskets

Baskets can hold many wonderful surprises. You can fill them with toiletries or makeup; small kitchen gadgets; food—such as a ham or turkey, some crackers, cheese, candy, jelly, jam, or baked goods; tools; games; books; clothes; flowers; or other items. Some of the nicest gifts I've received have come in a basket. Here is an idea that will especially be appreciated.

Cookies and Cocoa Gift Basket

A few years ago, a neighbor surprised me with a basketful of homemade cookies. She included a homemade cocoa mix that was absolutely delicious. I was delighted! It made my Christmas extra special that year.

If you would like to consider using this idea for a Christmas gift, feel free to use any of the cookie recipes in chapter 9 and include the cocoa mix as an added bonus.

Materials

An attractive empty basket
1 or 2 Mason jars with lids and rings
    (The Mason jars can be small or large, depending
      on the size of the recipient's family.)
Cocoa mix (below)
Christmas wrapping paper or fabric
Decorative-edged scissors
Homemade cookies
A bow for the handle of the basket
Paper label (See pages 69–72.)
Christmas tissue paper (optional)
Christmas mugs (optional)

Cocoa Mix Recipe

1 cup powdered sugar
½ cup cocoa powder
½ cup non-dairy cream powder
¼ tsp. salt
2¾ cups instant nonfat powdered milk
1 cup miniature marshmallows, wrapped in pretty cellophane
    or placed in a baggie tied with a bow (optional)

Directions

Mix the dry cocoa ingredients together and pour them into one of the Mason jars. Securely place the lid and ring on the jar.

Cut a 10-inch-square piece from the Christmas wrapping paper (or fabric) and place it on the table, decorative side down. Turn the jar of cocoa mix upside down (lid first) and place it in the center of the wrapping paper. Draw the ends of the wrapping paper upward toward you. At the neck of the jar, wrap the ribbon around the wrapping paper and tie it in a pretty bow. Turn the jar right side up and place a label on it with directions on how to mix the cocoa, which is to add 3 to 4 tablespoons of the mix to 1 cup of hot water.

Bake the cookies, and when they've cooled, place them in a pretty container. You can decorate an empty Cool Whip container (or something similar), or place the cookies on a pretty disposable plate and cover them with decorative cellophane.

Place a couple of layers of Christmas tissue in the basket. Add the cookies, marshmallows, and cocoa mix. Tie a big bow on the handle of the basket. Don't forget to include a card!

You can also combine the dry cookie ingredients and put them in a jar. Label the jar with instructions, such as necessary additional ingredients, oven temperature, how to prepare the dough, and how to bake the cookies. If you do it this way, you will have room in the basket to add inexpensive Christmas mugs for each member of the recipient's family.

Crackers and Cheese Gift Basket

Fill a basket with a variety of crackers and cheeses. Add a carton of eggnog or juice. Decorate the basket and give it to someone special.

Ice Melter in a Bucket

My neighbors gave me one of these several Christmases ago, and I refill the bucket and reuse it every year. What a practical and thoughtful gift!

Materials

Empty gallon-sized bucket with lid (used or new)
Ice melter (to melt ice and snow on sidewalks and driveways)
Scoop (can be small and inexpensive)
Bow or other decoration
Spray paint (optional)

Directions

If your bucket is in really bad shape, you may want to spray paint it. You can also purchase a nice bucket at your local hardware store.

Fill the bucket with ice melter and bury the scoop in it so just a small portion of the handle is showing. Put the lid on the bucket. Attach a silk poinsettia or some other Christmas decoration to the top of the bucket. You'll be amazed at how appreciated this gift will be!

Ice melter in a bucket

Bath Salts

Materials

1 cup Epsom Salts
⅛ tsp. food coloring
2 tsp. baking soda
½ tsp. fragrance oil (optional)
2 tsp. glycerin (optional)
Decorative bottle
Mixing bowl that won't stain
Mixing spoon that won't stain
Ribbon or other decorations
Label (See pages 69–72.)
Spray paint (optional)

Bath salts

Directions

To accurately measure the amount of salt you will need, fill the decorative bottle with Epsom Salts. Once you have completely filled the bottle, pour the salt from the bottle into a measuring cup and measure it into a mixing bowl. Add the correct amount of baking soda, food coloring, fragrance oil (if desired), and glycerin (if desired). Thoroughly mix everything together until the color is well distributed. Variation: Add ¼ cup sea salt and ¾ cup Epsom Salts instead of 1 cup Epsom Salts.

Once the desired color and aroma are achieved, use a funnel to pour the salt back into the bottle. Add ribbons, bows, or other decorations. Attach a label (see pages 69–72) to the bottle with the instructions of how much salt to use, which is ⅓ to ½ cup of salt to a tubful of water.

Tip: If the lid of the bottle has any undesirable markings, spray paint it before putting it on the bottle.

Heating Pad

Materials

Heating pad

Soft hand towel (or similar material)
Rice
Sewing thread to match hand towel
Gift tag (See pages 69–72.)

Directions

Everyone loves these! They are soothing on stiff joints and muscles. The heating pad needs to fit into a microwave to be warmed, so don't make it too big.

Fold the dish towel in half and sew two of the sides closed. (Or you can double the material by folding the towel in half twice.) Fill ⅔ full of rice. Add more rice if desired, but don't overfill; the rice needs to be loose inside of the bag. Fold the edges of the third side into the bag and hand baste it closed. On a sewing machine with a decorative stitch, sew a seam around all four edges. Remove any hand basting if necessary. Add a gift tag (pages 69–72) with instructions on how long to leave the heating pad in the microwave (usually 1 to 2 minutes on medium heat).

Homemade Candles

Refer to page 26 for candle making instructions. It is always nice to receive a candle as a gift, but a homemade candle is even better!

Advent Calendar

Refer to page 22 for the instructions and patterns for making an advent calendar. This is especially a hit in families with small children.

Oven Mitt and Poems

Buy an oven mitt (or make one yourself with nonflammable material) and attach to it one of the poems on the following page. Roll the printed poem into a scroll, secure it with a pretty ribbon, and present it with your gift. In one of the poems, the words "special gift" are substituted for "oven mitt" so you can include the optional poem with your gift of a hot pad, an apron, or anything else to do with baking.

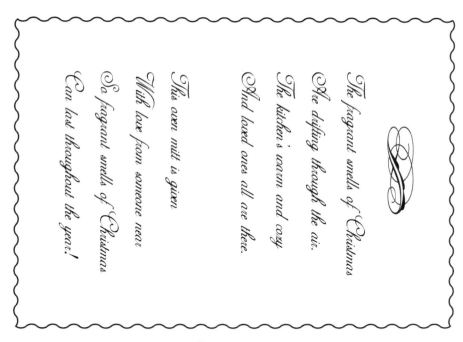

The fragrant smells of Christmas
Are drifting through the air.
The kitchen's warm and cozy
And loved ones all are there.

This oven mitt is given
With love from someone near
So fragrant smells of Christmas
Can last throughout the year!

Oven mitt poem

Cut out the poem, roll it into a scroll, secure it with
a pretty ribbon, and present it with a gift to someone special.

Optional poem

The fragrant smells of Christmas
Are drifting through the air.
The kitchen's warm and cozy
And loved ones all are there.

This special gift is given
With love from someone near
So fragrant smells of Christmas
Can last throughout the year!

Refrigerator Magnets

I love refrigerator magnets, and I always enjoy receiving them from my friends.

Type a favorite saying on your computer. Print it on nice paper, decorate it, and add a small magnet to the back. (You can purchase sheets of magnet from any craft store.) The recipient will more than likely attach it to her refrigerator where it will keep her sane on difficult days!

Use candy molds (see page 12) to make plaster of paris shapes. (Or mix up a batch of salt dough.) Paint and decorate the shapes, and when they are dry, securely fasten a strong magnet to the back of each one. Give the magnet to a friend for Christmas. She will love it!

Attach a photo of your child to a piece of nice paper. Add the child's name and a special message. Glue a magnet to the back of the paper and give it to Grandma and Grandpa for Christmas.

Snow Globes

I have received a lot of nice comments about the snow globes on page 28. People seem to be fascinated with them. Try making one for each of your neighbors, especially those with children. They will be pleased!

Handmade Ornaments

Any one of the handmade ornaments in chapter 2 (page 3) would make an excellent gift. I know a family that makes ornaments each year for everyone in the neighborhood. I have all their ornaments on my tree, and I look forward to receiving one from them again next year.

Family Cookbook

Collect a favorite recipe (or two) from each of your relatives' families and combine the recipes into a simple, inexpensive cookbook. Give a copy to everyone for Christmas.

Family Photo Calendar

Take candid photos of your family throughout the year. If you don't have a digital camera, you'll have to scan your photos into files on your computer. If you don't have access to a scanner, you can always have them scanned professionally; however, check the prices first, because it can be expensive.

Once you have your photos in your computer, print copies of them and either paste them onto an existing calendar, or design a calendar of your own and add photos to it. Give a copy of the calendar to each member of your family.

Children's Handprints

Buy plaster of paris and make prints of your children's hands and feet. The instructions are usually on the container. Grandma and Grandpa will love it!

Personalized Towels

Purchase an inexpensive towel and embroider, sew, or paint the recipient's name on it.

Personalized Pillowcases and Pillows

Purchase a pillowcase and embroider, sew, or paint the recipient's name on it. Keep your design simple, because it's hard to sleep on something that's lumpy, bumpy, or rough. For an added extra touch, purchase a pillow to go with it.

Handmade Jewelry

Beads are inexpensive and beaded jewelry is easy to make. You can even purchase beads with the letters of the alphabet on them so you can add the recipient's name on each piece.

Make necklaces and bracelets by repeating the suggested bead patterns on pages 15 and 16 (or make up your own patterns). Not only do they make beautiful ornaments, but they also make beautiful jewelry.

Family Histories

Choose a family member who has passed away and write his history. (Or you can choose someone who is still alive.) Collect photos of this person and add the photos to his written history. Better yet, if he is still alive, electronically record a conversation with him. Make copies for everyone in your family.

Candy Bar Wrappers

These are especially fun. I have included patterns on the following pages for the two most popular sizes of candy bars (8 oz. and 1.45 oz.). Color and decorate the graphics, cut the wrapper out on the trim marks, and glue or tape it to a candy bar. What a sweet treat!

Additional Gift Suggestions

Here are a few more ideas:

1. Children's artwork, framed
2. Journals
3. Deck of cards with rule book
4. Collage of family photos
5. Popcorn (popped or unpopped)
6. Cake, muffin, or cookie mix with appropriate pan
7. Stationery
8. Board games
9. Screwdriver or small tool set
10. Peanut butter or jelly (add a bow or a nice wrapping on the lid) with a fresh loaf of bread

May your holidays be bright

Merry Christmas!

8 oz. candy bar wrapper
Enlarge to 140 percent (A CD-ROM containing the full-sized
pattern is available at www.cedarfort.com.)

And she brought forth her firstborn son, and wrapped him in swaddling clothes, and laid him in a manger; because there was no room for them in the inn.
Luke 2:7

8 oz. candy bar wrapper
Enlarge to 140 percent (A CD-ROM containing the full-sized
pattern is available at www.cedarfort.com.)

Happy Holidays!

And a Prosperous New Year!

8 oz. candy bar wrapper
Enlarge to 140 percent (A CD-ROM containing the full-sized
pattern is available at www.cedarfort.com.)

Wise men still seek him

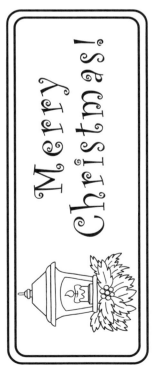

May all your Christmas dreams come true!

1.45 oz. candy bar wrappers

Enlarge to 120 percent (A CD-ROM containing the full-sized pattern is available at www.cedarfort.com.)

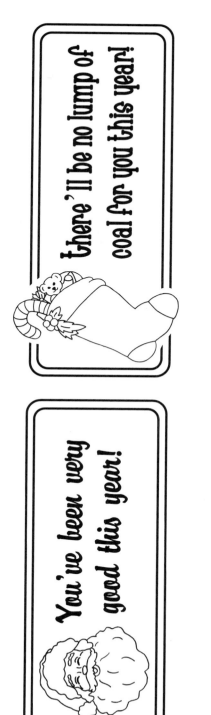

there'll be no lump of coal for you this year!

you've been very nice!

You've been very good this year!

Merry Christmas from Santa Claus

1.45 oz. candy bar wrappers

Enlarge to 120 percent (A CD-ROM containing the full-sized pattern is available at www.cedarfort.com.)

Chapter Six
Wrap It up

Nothing is more tedious than wrapping gifts! Isn't there a way to make it fun?

How about designing your own wrappings? They don't need to be expensive—just creative. Children especially enjoy doing this, and it's always a good idea to get your children involved.

Gifts don't always have to be wrapped.

Homemade Wrapping Paper

It doesn't matter what kind of paper you use when you make your own wrapping paper. It's what you do with the paper that makes the wrapping special. You can use a roll of brown parcel (or packing) paper, butcher paper, paper sacks that have been cut apart, old calendars, pretty material (such as old sheets, blankets, skirts, dresses, nightgowns, or robes), or discarded maps. Decorate the wrapping paper using the following suggested methods. You'll need newspapers to place under your work so you won't have to spend a lot of time cleaning up. Protect your children's clothing by covering them with old adult-size shirts or aprons. You'll also need plenty of wet rags or dishcloths to wipe those messy little hands!

Homemade Finger Paint

This recipe has been around for years. My second grade teacher would mix up a batch of red, yellow, green, and blue finger paint and bring it to school for us to use in our art class. It's simple to make and a lot of fun for children.

Bring ¾ cups of water to a boil. Dissolve ¼ cup cornstarch in a small amount of cold water (just like making gravy, only without the bullion). Add the cold water and cornstarch mixture to the boiling water. (If you don't dissolve the cornstarch in cold water first, your paint will be lumpy.) Continue to boil your finger paint mixture until it is clear and thick. Take it off the heat and add food coloring. The more food coloring you add, the brighter the colors will be. You can also add a little dry poster paint (tempera) powder to make your colors brighter. Flour can be used in place of cornstarch, but you'll need to add a lot more flour to make it the right consistency.

Cookie Cutter Stamps

Mix up a batch of homemade finger paint and pour each color onto a separate plate. Choose your favorite Christmas cookie cutter, preferably a plastic one with thick top edges. You'll be using the flat top side of your cookie cutter instead of the sharp bottom side that you would normally use to cut shapes in your cookie dough.

Dip the cookie cutter into the paint, making sure that all of the edges are covered. Using the cutter as a stamp, push the paint onto the wrapping paper so that all of the edges of the cutter are touching the paper. Before the paint dries, sprinkle your design with glitter. The recipient will love the gift (and the wrapping paper)!

Sponge Stamps

Purchase some inexpensive sponges from your local department store, or use old ones that are already available in your home. Copy and reduce in size the cookie cutter patterns found on pages 93–102 and trace them with a fine-tipped marker onto the sponges. (Or you can make and trace your own patterns.) Once you've traced the patterns onto your sponges, cut the shapes out of the sponges, dip the sponge shapes into the paint, and stamp the sponge patterns onto the paper. Sprinkle glitter onto the paint before it dries so that your design will sparkle.

Raw Potato Stamps

Cut a raw potato in half and push your favorite Christmas cookie cutter into the potato. Cut away the excess potato from around the imprint.

(The end of the potato should look similar to the stamping end of a rubber stamp.) Dip the imprint end of the potato into your paint and press it onto the wrapping paper. If you want your design to sparkle, then sprinkle glitter onto the imprint before the paint dries.

Sidewalk Chalk Designs

Children love sidewalk chalk. Let them use it to draw Christmas designs onto your future wrapping paper. Spray the designs with hairspray and let the hairspray dry. The chalk will stay on the paper, and the recipients will be extra happy with their gifts on Christmas morning.

Stencil Decorations

Trace a cookie cutter (or one of the patterns on pages 93–102) onto a piece of thin cardboard (or card stock) and cut the shape of the cookie cutter out of the cardboard. Show your children how to lay the cardboard onto the paper and color the opening with paint, markers, or a glue stick (for glitter). Be creative with your patterns, and watch your wrapping paper become extraordinary!

Paper Sack Gift Bags

Instead of wrapping your gifts, why not decorate paper sacks and use them as gift bags? The time spent will be part of the offering, and the recipient will appreciate it even more. You can spray paint your sack or use any of the above decorating methods to make a plain paper bag special. If you want to add ribbon or yarn for a handle, fold the top edges of the sack down a couple of times (at least 1 inch with each fold) and punch holes where you want to attach the handle. Tie ribbon or yarn to the sack, and presto—you have a handle. You can also use decorative-edged scissors or punches around the top edge of the sack, which will make your gift bag even more attractive. Decorate your bag with glitter, buttons, stamps, stickers, beads, felt, photos, stencils, ribbon, or any other embellishment that looks nice.

Manila Envelope Gift Bags

If you have an old manila envelope on hand, or if you want to buy a box of them (they are much less expensive than wrapping paper or gift bags), you can make your own gift bag by cutting the flap end off and making three simple folds along the sides and bottom of the envelope. The larger the envelope, the larger the bag will be.

Start by cutting off the top flap end of the envelope. (See figure 1.)

Measure and lightly mark 1½ inches in on the sides and bottom of the envelope. (See figure 1.) You can measure in farther if you want, depending on how broad and deep you want your bag. The bottom and two sides must be measured equally for this to work.

On your measured marks (or on the dotted lines in figure 1), fold the bottom and the two sides, making sure that your folds are all the way across the envelope. For versatility, you will need to make the folds in both directions, forward and backward along the lines. Some people prefer to score the envelope instead of folding it, but it weakens the envelope so that it tears more easily.

Put your left hand (or right hand if you are left handed) into the envelope. Using your right hand, push one of the sides of the envelope inward against your left hand. Use your premeasured folds to flatten the first side of the gift bag so that it forms the side of a box. (See figure 2.) The bottom end of the side of the bag should form a triangle that is horizontal to the bottom of the bag. (See figures 3 and 4.) Repeat this procedure for the other side. This may take some practice, but it will seem easy once you get used to it.

Using a glue gun, glue the triangular flaps to the bottom of the bag. (See figure 5.) You're now ready to

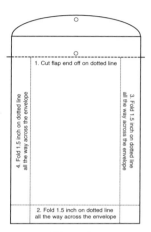

Figure 1

Figure 2

Figure 3

Figure 4

Figure 5

Figure 6   Figure 7

decorate. (See figure 6.) If necessary, erase your pencil markings before you begin decorating.

If you want to add a handle, you must reinforce the sides of the bag. To do this, glue cardboard along the inside sides of the bag before you punch the holes for the handle.

The gift bag in figure 7 was spray painted and decorated with lace, pinecones, silk leaves, and other embellishments. The handle was beaded, and the top was edged with decorative-edged scissors.

If your bag is large enough, you can also use it for a luminary. (See chapter 13, page 164.)

Gift Baskets

If you are in a hurry and all else fails, you can always purchase inexpensive baskets from your local dollar store, add decorations, tissue paper, and a bow, and present your gift in a beautiful personalized basket. (See page 51.)

Gift Tags

It's fun and easy to make your own gift tags. Use card stock, or you can even cut squares from wrapping paper. Decorate your tags with markers, paint, glitter, stickers, stamps, or ribbon. Add the recipient's name and sign your own. That's all there is to it! For your convenience, I've included a few gift tags on the following pages.

To: _____

From: _____

To: _____

From: _____

To: _____

From: _____

To: _____

From: _____

Instructions: _____

_____

_____

_____

_____

Just For You

To: _____

From: _____

Instructions:

_____

_____

_____

Merry Christmas!

To: _____

From: _____

Instructions: _____

_____

_____

_____

_____

Peace

To: _____

From: _____

A Special Note

_____

_____

_____

_____

Chapter Seven
Gone but Never Forgotten:
Remembering Deceased Loved Ones

*B*ecause of my faith in God, I know I will eventually be reunited with my deceased loved ones. That is why my family and I continue to involve them in our lives. The loss of a loved one is never easy, but it helps to remember that they are still with us in spirit.

Decorating the Grave of a Loved One

It is a tradition for our family to decorate my father's and brothers' graves every year at Christmastime. It's seldom expensive, and we try to remember them as we do those members of our family who are still alive.

When my brother died, my father planted an evergreen bush next to his grave. When circumstances allow, we collect our silk flowers and ornaments and decorate the bush. We have also purchased wreaths for each deceased member of our family, and we hang them securely on their gravestones with a wreath hanger or a strong wire that has been bent to form a hook. We've used the same wreaths and silk poinsettias for years, and they are still in excellent condition.

I can only remember one time when some of our flowers disappeared. Because it was so windy that year, we're still not sure whether they were stolen or if they just blew away. If you secure your decorations, you won't need to worry about the wind relocating them or causing them to fall and break. It's also a good idea not to decorate with anything that cannot withstand the harsh elements of winter.

Christmas Eve Graveside Candlelight Ceremony

One of our family's favorite traditions is to light candles and luminaries and place them on our loved ones' graves on Christmas Eve. Several acquaintances of ours have been doing this for years, but it wasn't until my father passed away that our family adopted the tradition. Since that time, we've noticed that many other families have also begun to participate.

Because it is usually cold in December, the first thing we do is make sure we are dressed properly. We learned quickly that if we want to enjoy this activity, we need to be warm.

When we arrive at the cemetery on Christmas Eve, we light our prepared candles and luminaries and place them on our loved ones' graves. We sing a Christmas carol, have a prayer, and each person in attendance is given an opportunity to express his feelings. We then sing a few more Christmas carols, read Luke 2:1–20 and Matthew 2:1–15, and end our ceremony with another prayer. After we have blown out the candles and the luminaries, we go to a designated home for dinner, games, and a movie. We never tire of this ritual, and we wouldn't want to spend our Christmas Eve in any other way.

If your city does not have an open cemetery on Christmas Eve, contact a member of your city council or attend one of their meetings and request that it be left open. This activity is time well spent, and you'll never feel closer to your departed loved ones than at their gravesides on Christmas Eve.

Individual and Family Histories

Another way to honor a deceased loved one is to write his history and give it to other family members as a Christmas gift. It can be the history of an individual, or it can be the history of his entire family. In either case, you can't go wrong by giving a gift of memories!

Chapter Eight
Preserving Memories

*D*o you remember any of the gifts you received for Christmas when you were a child? Do you remember what you did to celebrate the holiday season? Have you ever taken part in a Christmas Nativity or written a letter to Santa Claus? If so, have you—or did you—do anything to preserve those memories? Most of us can't remember what we did or received last year, let alone ten or twenty years ago. You can never take too many photos or record too many details when it comes to the holiday season and your family and friends!

Creating a Christmas Memory Book

The following is a short list of things that make good memories. I've included a cover suggestion on page 77 for a Christmas memory book. I've also included a journal page on page 78. If you want, you can copy these pages and add graphics or decorations to make them more personal. Remember that the best scrapbook is an individually unique scrapbook, and the more of your personal self that goes into it, the better it will be!

1. Baby's first Christmas
2. Letters to Santa Claus
3. Wish lists (Even if you don't receive what you wished for, it's still fun to wish!)
4. Traditions kept
5. Christmas cards received
6. Gifts received and who gave them to you
7. Parties attended (including New Year's Eve)

8. Photos of decorations, inside and outside your home
9. Photos of the weather. Did it snow? Did anyone build a snowman?
10. Photos of plays, choirs, nativities, and caroling parties in which family members participated
11. What was on the menu for Christmas Eve, Christmas Day, and New Year's Eve?
12. Photos of new hairstyles, new outfits, new shoes, or new jewelry
13. Memories and photos of your family pets
14. Who was your teenage son or daughter dating? Were there any special holiday dates?
15. Did anyone become engaged on Christmas?
16. Did anyone get married during the holiday season?
17. Were any babies born?
18. Did you enjoy a special date with your spouse, boyfriend, or girlfriend?
19. What movies did you see? Which movie was your favorite?
20. Do you have a favorite Christmas hymn or song?
21. What car were you driving?
22. Did you visit any relatives?
23. Did anyone special pass away? It may be extremely painful now, but photos and recorded feelings will be a comfort to you later.
24. Did you anonymously help someone in need?
25. Were you a secret Santa to anyone?
26. Did you do something extra special for someone?
27. Did you volunteer in any way?
28. Did you hear from someone you haven't heard from in years?
29. Did anything spiritual happen that was out of the ordinary?
30. What was the happiest moment, the most spiritual experience, your favorite gift, or your best memory of the holiday season?

Family Videos

Another great way to celebrate Christmas and preserve a memory is to videotape your family as they go about their lives during the holiday season. Not everyone can afford a camera, but it's a lot of fun for those who can. It's also fun to get together with your family at a later date and watch the completed video. Having copies made isn't as expensive as it used to be, and most family members would be pleased to receive a copy for Christmas the following year. Remember that preserving memories doesn't have to be expensive—it just has to be fun!

Christmas
Memories

Chapter Nine
Tasty Treats

*C*hristmas is never complete without the heavenly aroma of goodies baking in the oven. Not only are they fun to eat, but they are also fun to share, and nothing gladdens the heart of a good neighbor like a plate of warm chocolate chip cookies. The following recipes are easy to make and delicious to eat. Just make sure you keep some for yourself!

Easy Chocolate and Caramel Pretzel Sticks

2 (14 oz.) pkgs. caramels
1 (12 oz.) pkg. pretzel rods or sticks
4 (8 oz.) milk chocolate candy bars
Decorating candy sprinkles

Chocolate and caramel pretzel sticks in gift bags

Butter (or spray with Pam) two large cookie sheets. Place the caramels in a microwave-safe dish and microwave on medium until the caramels are melted together and runny (approximately 2 to 3 minutes). Don't overcook the caramels, or your pretzel sticks will be hard instead of chewy.

Stir the caramel well. Dip the pretzels into the melted caramel, leaving 2 inches of the sticks uncovered. Place the pretzel sticks on the buttered cookie sheets. Cover with waxed paper and set aside for 30 minutes or until the caramel has solidified. Carefully remove the pretzel sticks from the cookie sheet with a metal spatula.

While the caramel is solidifying, break the chocolate bars into medium-sized pieces and place them in a microwave-safe dish. With the microwave on medium, melt the chocolate one minute at a time, stirring it after each minute until it is runny. Don't overcook the chocolate, or your pretzel sticks will be hard instead of chewy.

Dip the caramel-covered pretzels into the melted chocolate, leaving 2 inches of the sticks uncovered. Place the sticks on the buttered cookie sheets and immediately sprinkle with decorating candy.

When the chocolate has completely solidified (approximately 2 hours), place the pretzel sticks into plastic gift bags (see photo) and tie them with a bow. (Yield: 2 dozen)

Santa's Favorite Soft Sugar Cookies

1 cup softened margarine
1½ cups sugar
2 eggs
¾ cup sour cream
2 tsp. vanilla extract
4 cups flour
1 tsp. baking powder
1 tsp. baking soda
1 tsp. salt

Santa's Favorite Soft Sugar Cookies

Cream together the margarine and sugar. Add the eggs, sour cream, and vanilla and beat well. Sift the dry ingredients together and add them to the combined wet mixture. Blend well. Chill the dough for one hour.

Roll the dough out on a floured surface and use the patterns provided on pages 93–102 (or your own cookie cutters) to cut the dough into shapes. Place the shapes on a cookie sheet and bake at 375 degrees for 10 to 15 minutes or until light golden brown. Don't overbake. Cover and let cool. (Yield: 3 dozen)

Sugar Cookie Icing

½ cup vegetable shortening
½ cup butter or cubed margarine

(*Continued on following page*)

Sugar Cookie Icing *(continued from previous page)*

    1 tsp. vanilla extract
    4 cups sifted powdered sugar
    2 Tbsp. canned evaporated milk (or regular milk)
    Food coloring (if desired)

Blend together the above ingredients, adding more milk if necessary. Beat the icing for 2 minutes with an electric mixer. Add food coloring if desired. Ice and decorate cookies.

Christmas Eve Scones and Honey Butter

    ¼ cup warm water   1 cup warm milk
    ½ Tbsp. yeast   1 tsp. salt
    ⅛ cup sugar   3–4 cups flour
    ⅛ cup shortening

Mix warm water, yeast, and sugar in a large bowl and let it sit for 5 to 10 minutes. Add the shortening, warm milk, and salt, and mix them all together. Start adding flour a little at a time until dough is moderately stiff. Turn out onto a lightly floured surface and knead until smooth and elastic (8 to 10 minutes by hand or 5 minutes in a mixing bowl with a dough hook). Transfer to a lightly oiled bowl, cover with plastic wrap, and let rise until doubled in size (approximately 1 hour). You can also place the dough in a plastic bag and leave it in the fridge overnight. Cut the dough into serving pieces and shape the pieces with your hands. Fry the scones (on both sides) in ½ to 1 inch of oil on medium heat until they are golden brown. (Caution: If the oil begins to smoke, turn off the heat and get your frying pan off the burner right away.) Serve immediately with honey butter and soup or chili. (Yield: 15 [3"] scones)

Honey Butter

    ½ cup butter (no substitutes)
    ½ cup honey
    ¼ tsp. vanilla extract

Mix the butter, honey, and vanilla extract together and beat them well with an electric mixer. Serve on warm scones.

Award-winning Chocolate Chip Cookies

Cream together: 1 cup Canola oil (or vegetable oil)
     ¾ cups brown sugar
     1 cup granulated sugar
     2 eggs
     2 tsp. vanilla extract
Sift together: 3 cups flour (or 2 cups
      flour and 2 cups oats)
     1 tsp. salt
     1 tsp. baking soda
Add: Chocolate Chips (or M&Ms®) and nuts

Award-winning
Chocolate Chip Cookies

Add the dry ingredients to the creamed mixture and use your hands to blend the dough well. (If you want to add 2 cups of oats, add them now.) Add desired amount of chocolate chips (or M&Ms®) and nuts, and bake at 375 degrees for 8 to 10 minutes or until light golden brown. Don't overbake. (Yield: 2 dozen)

Traditional Mint Brownies

Brownies

⅔ cup butter or margarine
4 oz. semi-sweet baking chocolate
   (Substitution: ⅓ cup cocoa
   or ⅔ cup chocolate chips)
1⅓ cups sugar
3 eggs
2 tsp. vanilla extract
4 tsp. honey (optional)
1 cup flour
½ tsp. salt
1 tsp. baking powder
1 cup chopped walnuts (optional)

Mint Frosting

⅓ cup butter or margarine
1 Tbsp. light corn syrup
½ tsp. peppermint extract
⅛ tsp. salt
2⅓ cups powdered sugar
1 to 2 Tbsp. milk
3 drops green food coloring

Chocolate Topping

¾ cup semi-sweet chocolate
   chips
3 Tbsp. butter or margarine

Traditional Mint
Brownies and No-bake
Shaggy Dawgs
(See page 91 for the
Shaggy Dawg recipe.)

Brownie Instructions

Place the butter and chocolate in a microwave-safe bowl and micro-wave one minute at a time, stirring after each minute until completely melted. Stir until smooth. Allow mixture to cool but don't let it harden.

In a separate bowl, cream together the sugar and eggs. Add the choc-olate mixture, vanilla extract, and honey (if desired). Sift the flour, salt, and baking powder together and add them to the combined mixture. Add nuts if desired. Mix all ingredients together until thoroughly blended. Pour into greased and floured 9 x 9 baking pan and bake for 30 minutes at 350 degrees. Don't overbake. Cool for at least 1 hour. (Yield: 1 dozen)

Mint Frosting Instructions

Melt the butter in the microwave and combine it with the corn syrup, peppermint extract, and salt. Blend in the powdered sugar ½ cup at a time and beat until smooth. Add milk if necessary. Beat in the green food coloring until the desired shade is achieved. Frost the cooled brownies. Cover and chill for 1 hour. (Tip: This frosting is also delicious on sugar cookies.)

Chocolate Topping Instructions

Pour the chocolate chips into a microwave-safe bowl. Add the butter and microwave on high one minute at a time until the chocolate melts. Stir until smooth. Pour the chocolate over the brownies and smooth it with a spoon or a knife. Refrigerate 1 hour or until the topping hardens.

Delicious Fudge

1⅔ cups evaporated milk
1 cup butter or margarine
4 cups sugar
2 cups semi-sweet chocolate chips
1 pint marshmallow cream
1 tsp. vanilla extract
1 cup (or more if desired) chopped walnuts

Delicious Fudge

Combine the evaporated milk, butter, and sugar in a saucepan. Stir-ring constantly, cook the mixture until it reaches softball stage (236 degrees). Remove the mixture from the heat and add the chocolate chips, marshmallow cream, and vanilla extract. Add nuts. Pour fudge into a but-tered 9 x 13 baking pan. Refrigerate until firm and cut into small 1-inch pieces. (Yield: 117 pieces)

Grandpa's Famous Oatmeal Cookies
Courtesy of Grandpa Doug

Mix together and beat thoroughly:
    2¼ cups Canola oil
        (or vegetable oil)
    3 cups brown sugar
    1½ cups granulated sugar
    3 eggs
    ¼ cup water
    2 tsp. vanilla extract

Grandpa's Famous Oatmeal Cookies

Sift together and add to above ingredients:
    3 cups flour
    3 tsp. salt
    1½ tsp. baking soda

Blend in:
    8 cups quick-cook oatmeal, added 2 cups at a time

Optional:
    Chocolate chips
        (or M&Ms®)
    Raisins
    Nuts

Using your hands, mix the ingredients together well. Add more water if necessary. If desired, add chocolate chips, M&Ms®, nuts, or raisins. Place the dough in balls on the cookie sheet and bake at 350 degrees for 12 to 15 minutes or until done. Don't overbake. (Yield: 5 dozen)

Caramel Popcorn
Courtesy of Nicole Chamberlain

4 bags microwave popping corn
    (12 cups popped)*
½ cup butter or margarine
1 cup light corn syrup

1 cup brown sugar
½ tsp. salt
1 tsp. baking soda

Microwave the 4 bags of popping corn. Remove any unpopped kernels and pour the popped corn into a large bowl. Set the popcorn aside. In a saucepan on medium heat, melt butter and stir in corn syrup, brown sugar, and salt. Bring to a boil, stirring constantly, and simmer for 6 minutes. Remove mixture from heat. Stir in baking soda. Gradually pour over popped corn and mix together well. (Yield: 12 cups)

*Use 5 bags of popcorn (15 cups popped) to make it less sticky and sweet, and 3 bags (9 cups popped) for popcorn balls. Butter your hands before making popcorn balls so the popcorn doesn't stick to your hands.

Chocolate Marshmallow Bars

1 cup butter	2 Tbsp. honey (optional)
6 oz. semi-sweet baking chocolate (Substitution: ½ cup cocoa or 1 cup chocolate chips)	1¾ cups flour
	½ tsp. salt
	1½ tsp. baking powder
	1 cup chopped walnuts (optional)
2 cups granulated sugar	1 (16 oz.) bag of miniature
4 eggs	marshmallows
2 tsp. vanilla extract	

Place the butter and chocolate in a microwave-safe bowl and microwave one minute at a time, stirring after each minute until completely melted. Stir until smooth. Allow mixture to cool but don't let it harden.

In a separate bowl, cream together the sugar and eggs. Add the chocolate mixture, vanilla extract, and honey (if desired). Sift the flour, salt, and baking powder together and add them to the combined mixture. Mix all ingredients together until thoroughly blended. Add nuts if desired.

Pour into a greased and floured 9 x 13 baking pan and bake for 35 to 40 minutes at 350 degrees. Don't overbake. Remove from oven and top with miniature marshmallows. With oven on broil, place bars back into the oven for approximately 1 minute or until the marshmallows are melted. Watch the marshmallows closely so they don't burn. Remove from oven and let cool. Ice bars with Chocolate Frosting below. (Yield: 2 dozen)

Chocolate Frosting

2½ Tbsp. flour	¼ cup butter	2 tsp. vanilla extract
½ cup milk	¼ cup shortening	2 lbs. powdered sugar
¼ tsp. salt	1 cup chocolate chips	

Blend together flour and milk. Cook on medium heat, stirring constantly until the mixture thickens. Mix in salt and set aside to cool.

Meanwhile, in a microwave-safe bowl, melt together the butter, shortening, and chocolate chips. Microwave one minute at a time, stirring after each minute until completely melted. Stir until smooth. Combine with cooled flour mixture and add vanilla extract. Add ¼ cup of the powdered sugar and blend well. Add more powdered sugar to make desired consistency. Beat with hand mixer until light and fluffy. Spread frosting on bars. (Tip: For vanilla icing, leave out the chocolate chips.)

Family Favorite Fruit Salad
Courtesy of Laura H. White

With an electric hand mixer, cream together:

    1½ cups cream cheese, softened

    ½ cup sugar

    ½ cup mayonnaise

Add and cream together with hand mixer:

    2 cups Cool Whip

    4 drops red food coloring

Family Favorite Fruit Salad

Stirring gently with a spoon, add:

    2 (12 oz.) pkgs. frozen strawberries, partially thawed

    1 (16 oz.) can crushed pineapple, thoroughly drained

    1½ cups colored miniature marshmallows

    Decorating candy sprinkles

      Pour into a 9 x 13 baking dish. Place miniature marshmallows on top in desired pattern and garnish with decorating candy sprinkles. Freeze for 6 hours and thaw for ½ hour before serving. (Yield: 16 servings)

Traditional Gingerbread House

Materials

Candy for decorating

Cake Decorating tips: star tip
    #21 (to attach walls and
    roof), star tip #32 (for
    edging), and round tip #6
    (for outlining figures)

Icing bag and coupler

Large piece of cardboard (or
    a large cookie sheet) and
    enough aluminum foil to cover the cardboard

Undecorated gingerbread house

Ingredients

1 cup shortening	1 tsp. salt
1 cup molasses	1 tsp. baking soda
½ cup granulated sugar	1½ tsp. ground cinnamon
½ cup brown sugar	1 Tbsp. ground ginger
5 cups flour	

This recipe yields more than enough dough for all the gingerbread patterns included in this chapter.

Melt the shortening and soften the molasses in the microwave. Blend them together with the sugars. Sift together the flour, salt, baking soda, cinnamon, and ginger. Add the dry ingredients a little at a time to the creamed mixture and blend them well with your hands until the dough sticks together and forms a smooth ball. The dough will be stiff and dry, and the baked dough will be hard. It must be this way so your gingerbread house will be solid. You may want to keep a small container of milk close by and add one teaspoon of milk at a time if the dough gets too stiff or dry.

Roll out the dough to a ¼-inch thickness and use a table knife and the patterns on pages 89–91 to cut out the pieces of your gingerbread house. Or, if you prefer, you can use your own patterns. Place the pieces of the gingerbread house on a cookie sheet and bake at 375 degrees for 10 to 12 minutes. Watch it closely so it doesn't burn. Cool thoroughly.

Decorator's Icing

This icing recipe should not be eaten because of the raw eggs. If children are participating, use the Easy Gingerbread House for Children instructions and the Butter Cream Icing recipe on the following page, or substitute meringue powder for the egg whites.

While the gingerbread is cooling, combine 5 cups powdered sugar with ½ teaspoon cream of tartar. Beat 4 egg whites (or 8 tsp. of meringue powder mixed with 8 Tbsp. water) and 2 tsp. vanilla extract together and combine them with the powdered sugar mixture. Beat with an electric hand mixer until stiff. Add more powdered sugar if necessary. Tightly cover the icing so it won't dry out.

Decorating Your Gingerbread House

You'll need a lot of candy for decoration, such as M&Ms®, mints, gumdrops, and small candy canes.

Cover a large piece of cardboard (or an upside down cookie sheet) with aluminum foil to use as a base for your gingerbread house.

Decorated gingerbread house

When the gingerbread pieces have completely cooled, lay them on the table rough side up. (Always remember to turn the rough side of the gingerbread toward the inside of the house.)

Avoiding the roof area (or peaks), use star tip #21 to pipe a thick line of icing along all three edges of the front and back walls. Pipe a thick line of icing along the bottom edges of the two side walls.

Erect the back wall by attaching it with the pre-piped icing to the aluminum foil base. Attach one of the side walls to the back wall, and continue attaching each wall until all four walls are erected.

Pipe a thick line of icing along the top edge of the peaks of the front and back walls. Attach the roof pieces to the roof peaks. Pipe a strip of icing down the middle of the roof to attach the two roof pieces. Hold the house in place for a few minutes while the icing sets. This icing dries fast and is extremely tacky, so you shouldn't have any trouble erecting your house or getting it to stabilize quickly.

Attach the chimney to the roof and add the trees and small figures to the aluminum foil base by piping a thick line of icing along the bottom edge of each piece.

Decorate your gingerbread house with icing (using tip star tip #32 for edging and round tip #6 for outlining the figures) and Christmas candy.

Easy Gingerbread House for Children

Follow the instructions above using graham crackers instead of gingerbread for the walls and roof of the house. Sugar cones can be turned upside down and decorated with candy for Christmas trees. Life Savers or Starlight Mints can be used as wheels on graham cracker trains. Encourage your children to use their imaginations. The possibilities are endless!

Butter Cream Icing

This recipe is not as sticky as the decorator's icing and doesn't hold the crackers together as well, but it is delicious and perfect for little tasters.

½ cup shortening, softened	4 cups powdered sugar
½ cup margarine, softened	2 Tbsp. milk
2 tsp. vanilla extract	

Soften the butter and shortening and cream them together with the vanilla. Blend in the sugar one cup at a time, beating well with a hand mixer after each addition. Add the milk and continue to beat the icing until it is light and fluffy. Add more powdered sugar if necessary. Tightly cover the icing until you are ready to use it.

Chimney of gingerbread house (cut and bake 1)

All gingerbread patterns should be enlarged 110 percent or more, depending on how big you want your house.

(A CD-ROM containing the full-sized patterns is available at ww.cedarfort.com.)

Front and back of gingerbread house (cut and bake 2)

Do not cut out the windows and door. It may weaken the house. The broken lines are to be used as decorating suggestions only. Using a table knife, press the door and window patterns into the uncooked dough. Outline the baked patterns with icing.

Cut and bake 4 trees

Cut and bake 2 snowmen

Roof of gingerbread house (cut and bake 2)

Cut and
bake 2
gingerbread
boys

Cut and
bake 2
gingerbread
girls

Do not cut out the window

Side walls of gingerbread house (cut and bake 2)

No-bake Shaggy Dawgs
Courtesy of Laurie Hansen

¾ cup chocolate chips
⅓ cup butter or margarine
4 Tbsp. milk
2 cups powdered sugar

3 cups miniature marshmallows
2 cups sweetened flaked coconut
½ cup nuts (optional)

Place the butter and chocolate in a microwave-safe bowl. Microwave one minute at a time, stirring after each minute until completely melted. Blend until smooth. Allow to cool slightly, but don't let it harden.

Add the milk and then the powdered sugar to the chocolate mixture and blend well. Mix in the miniature marshmallows, coconut, and nuts. Place in a buttered 8 x 8 baking pan and chill for one hour. Cut into 1-inch pieces and serve. (Yield: 64 pieces)

Homemade Root Beer
Courtesy of Robert Haymond

1 (10 gal.) insulated water container with lid and spigot
5 gal. cold tap water
1 (1 gal.) empty plastic bottle for measuring
1 (5 lb.) bag fine granulated sugar

1 (2 fl. oz.) bottle McCormick root beer concentrate
1 (2 lit.) bottle A&W root beer (optional)*
6 lbs. dry ice (broken into small pieces)
Child's plastic garden shovel (approximately 26" in length) for
    mixing root beer

Start making the root beer at least 1 hour before it is to be served. If you don't have a 10-gallon container, reduce the quantities proportionally.

Using the 1-gallon plastic bottle to measure the water, pour the 5 gallons of cold tap water into the 10-gallon water container. Add the 5 pounds of sugar and use the child's plastic shovel to stir the mixture. Make sure the sugar is completely dissolved before adding the entire contents of the bottle of root beer concentrate.

Slowly add the dry ice pieces. Don't put the lid on the container at this time. Let the dry ice bubble until the fog has thinned. Use the plastic garden shovel to slightly stir the mixture to make sure the dry ice pieces are not sticking to the bottom of the container.

Place the lid ajar on the container and let the mixture bubble until it is to be served. (Yield: 5 gallons)

* If adding the 2-liter bottle of root beer, you will need to add 2 less liters of tap water. Instead of adding all 5 gallons of water at the same time, pour only 4 gallons into the 10-gallon container. When you add the 5th gallon of water, remove 2 liters of it by pouring it into the empty 2-liter bottle. Add the remaining water from the 5th gallon to the 10-gallon container. Add the A&W root beer when you add the root beer concentrate.

Peppermint Bark

1 (12 oz.) pkg. vanilla baking chips
½–1 tsp. peppermint extract (according to taste)
¼ tsp. red or green food coloring
½ cup crushed peppermint candies or candy canes

Melt chips in the microwave and blend until smooth. Add peppermint extract, food coloring, and crushed candy. Spread on large foil-lined baking sheet and refrigerate until set. Break into pieces and serve.

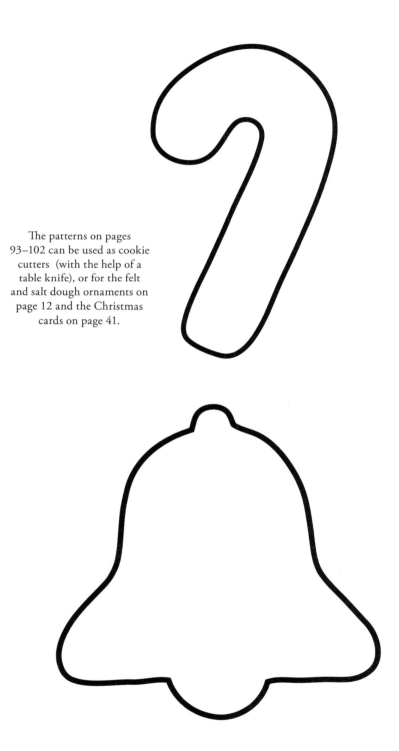

The patterns on pages 93–102 can be used as cookie cutters (with the help of a table knife), or for the felt and salt dough ornaments on page 12 and the Christmas cards on page 41.

Enlarge the alphabet patterns to at least 140 percent. (A CD-ROM containing the full-sized patterns is available at www.cedarfort.com.)

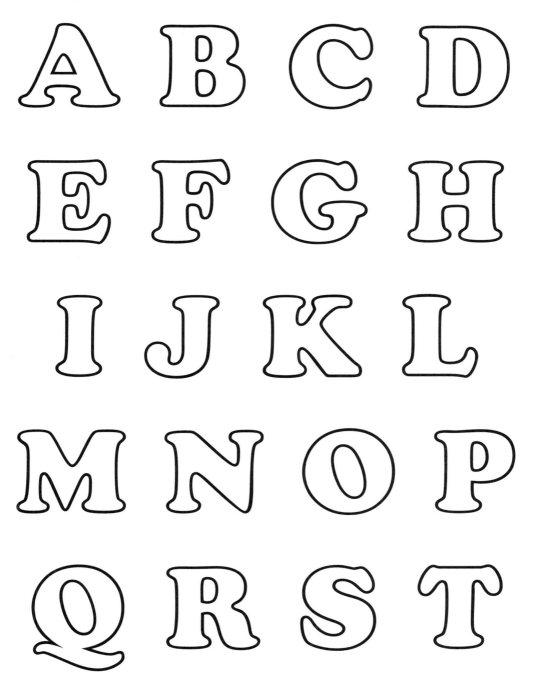

Alphabet for cookie cutters, plaster of paris and salt dough ornaments, advent calendar, and card designs

U V W

X Y Z

a b c d

e f g h

i j k l

m n o p

q r s t

u v w

x y z

1 2 3 4

Star of Bethlehem
cookie cutter

Chapter Ten
"Caroling, Caroling, Now We Go"

A caroling party can be fun—if it is organized and the participants are prepared.

The area in which you live may be cold in December, so dress accordingly. You will also need lyrics to the songs you plan on singing. And because it's usually dark during the time you will be caroling, you may want to bring flashlights.

The use of candles can be fun, but they are also dangerous. To help minimize the danger, you can always put them in clear glass mugs with handles. You can usually find the mugs at your local dollar store. Paper plates will work, but you'll still have an open flame. If you would like to use paper plates as candleholders, you will need to poke a hole through the plate and slide a 10- or 12-inch taper candle through the hole. Grasp the bottom end of the candle and rest the paper plate on your fist. This eliminates the possibility of wax drippings, and it also provides some protection from the flame. Just make sure you blow the candle out before the flame reaches the plate. Keep in mind that if it's windy, your candles aren't going to stay lit. That's why clear glass mugs with handles are your best option.

For refreshments, hot chocolate and apple cider are always a hit. Donuts and other finger foods are also recommended.

Most song lyrics are copyrighted, so it's not a good idea to make copies. Those carolers who have songbooks can always share them, but that may still leave some carolers out. I've included in this chapter the lyrics to several of our most beloved Christmas songs. Their copyrights have long ago expired, so you can make as many copies as you'd like.

Once your party is organized, set the date and go have fun!

A Collection of Traditional Christmas Carols

Joy to the World
Text: Isaac Watts, 1674–1748
Music: George F. Handel, 1685–1759

Joy to the world! the Lord is come;
Let earth receive her King;
Let every heart prepare Him room,
And Saints and angels sing,
And Saints and angels sing,
And Saints, and Saints and angels sing.

Rejoice! Rejoice when Jesus reigns,
And Saints their songs employ;
While fields and floods,
Rocks, hills, and plains
Repeat the sounding joy,
Repeat the sounding joy,
Repeat, repeat the sounding joy.

No more will sin and sorrow grow,
Nor thorns infest the ground;
He'll come and make the blessings flow
Far as the curse was found,
Far as the curse was found,
Far as, far as the curse was found.

He rules the world with truth and grace,
And makes the nations prove
The glories of His righteousness,
And wonders of His love,
And wonders of His love,
And wonders, wonders of His love.

Rejoice! Rejoice in the Most High,
While Israel spreads abroad
Like stars that glitter in the sky

And ever worship God
And ever worship God
And ever, and ever worship God.

O, Come, All Ye Faithful

Text and music: Attr. to John F. Wade, ca. 1711–1786

O, come, all ye faithful,
Joyful and triumphant,
O, come ye, O come ye to Bethlehem;
Come and behold him,
Born the King of angels;

Chorus:
O, come, let us adore him,
O, come, let us adore him,
O, come, let us adore him, Christ the Lord.

Sing, choirs of angels,
Sing in exultation,
Sing, all ye citizens of heaven above;
Glory to God
Glory In the highest

Repeat Chorus

Yea, Lord, we greet thee,
Born this happy morning;
Jesus, to thee be all glory given;
Word of the Father,
Now in flesh appearing

Repeat Chorus

Angels We Have Heard on High

Text and music: French carol, ca. 1862

Angels we have heard on high,
Sweetly singing o'er the plains,
And the mountains in reply
Echoing their joyous strains.

Gloria in excelsis Deo.
Gloria in excelsis Deo.

Shepherds, why this jubilee?
Why your joyous strains prolong?
What the gladsome tidings be
Which inspires your heav'nly song?
Gloria in excelsis Deo.
Gloria in excelsis Deo.

Come to Bethlehem and see
Him whose birth the angels sing;
Come, adore on bended knee
Christ, the Lord, the newborn King.
Gloria in excelsis Deo.
Gloria in excelsis Deo.

Silent Night
Text: Joseph Mohr, 1792–1848
Music: Franz Gruber, 1787–1863

Silent night, holy night,
All is calm, all is bright
Round yon virgin mother and child.
Holy infant so tender and mild,
Sleep in heavenly peace.
Sleep in heavenly peace.

Silent night, holy night,
Shepherds quake at the sight,
Glories stream from heaven afar,
Heav'nly hosts sing alleluia;
Christ, the Savior, is born!
Christ, the Savior, is born!

Silent night, holy night,
Son of God, love's pure light
Radiant beams from thy holy face,

With the dawn of redeeming grace,
Jesus, Lord, at thy birth.
Jesus, Lord, at thy birth.

Away in a Manger

Text: Anon., ca. 1883
Music: William J. Kirkpatrick, 1838–1921

Away in a manger, no crib for a bed,
The little Lord Jesus laid down his sweet head.
The stars in the heavens looked down where he lay,
The little Lord Jesus asleep on the hay.

The cattle are lowing, the poor baby wakes,
But little Lord Jesus no crying he makes.
I love thee, Lord Jesus! Look down from the sky,
And stay by my cradle till morning is nigh.

Be near me Lord Jesus, I ask thee to stay.
Close by me forever, and love me I pray.
Bless all the dear children, in thy tender care.
And lead us to heaven to live with thee there.

It Came upon the Midnight Clear

Text: Edmund H. Sears, 1810–1876
Music: Richard S. Willis, 1819–1900

It came upon the midnight clear,
That glorious song of old,
From angels bending near the earth,
To touch their harps of gold!
"Peace on the earth, good will to men,
From heaven's all gracious King!"
The world in solemn stillness lay,
To hear the angels sing.

Still through the cloven skies they come,
With peaceful wings unfurled,

And still their heavenly music floats,
O'er all the weary world;
Above its sad and lowly plains,
They bend on hovering wing.
And ever o'er its Babel sounds,
The blessed angels sing.

For lo! the days are hastening on,
By prophets seen of old,
When with the ever-circling years,
Shall come the time foretold,
When the new heav'n and earth shall own
The Prince of Peace their King,
And the whole world sends back the song,
Which now the angels sing.

O Little Town of Bethlehem

Text: Phillips Brooks, 1835–1893
Music: Lewis H. Redner, 1831–1908

O little town of Bethlehem,
How still we see thee lie!
Above thy deep and dreamless sleep
The silent stars go by;
Yet in thy dark streets shineth
The everlasting Light;
The hopes and fears of all the years
Are met in thee tonight.

For Christ is born of Mary,
And gathered all above,
While mortals sleep, the angels keep
Their watch of wondering love.
O morning stars, together
Proclaim the holy birth!
And praises sing to God the King,
And peace to men on earth.

How silently, how silently,
The wondrous gift is given!
So God imparts to human hearts
The blessings of his heaven.
No ear may hear his coming,
But in this world of sin,
Where meek souls will receive him, still
The dear Christ enters in.

O holy Child of Bethlehem!
Descend to us, we pray.
Cast out our sin and enter in,
Be born in us today.
We hear the Christmas angels
The great glad tidings tell;
O come to us, abide with us,
Our Lord Emmanuel!

Hark! The Herald Angels Sing

Text: Charles Wesley, 1707–1788
Music: Felix Mendelssohn, 1809–1847

Hark! the herald angels sing
Glory to the newborn King!
Peace on earth and mercy mild,
God and sinners reconciled!
Joyful, all ye nations, rise,
Join the triumph of the skies;
With th' angelic host proclaim
Christ is born in Bethlehem!
Hark! the herald angels sing
Glory to the newborn King!

Hail! The heav'n-born Prince of Peace!
Hail! The Son of righteousness!
Light and life to all He brings,
Ris'n with healing in his wings.
Mild He lays His glory by,

Born that man no more may die;
Born to raise the sons of earth,
Born to give them second birth.
Hark! The herald angels sing
Glory to the newborn king.

We Wish You a Merry Christmas

Traditional English Carol, date unknown
Text and Music: Anon.

We wish you a Merry Christmas,
We wish you a Merry Christmas,
We wish you a Merry Christmas and a Happy New Year.
Good tidings we bring to you and your kin;
Good tidings for Christmas and a Happy New Year.

Oh, bring us some figgy pudding;
Oh, bring us some figgy pudding;
Oh, bring us some figgy pudding and a cup of good cheer
Good tidings we bring to you and your kin;
Good tidings for Christmas and a Happy New Year.

We won't go until we get some,
We won't go until we get some,
We won't go until we get some, so bring some right here
Good tidings we bring to you and your kin;
Good tidings for Christmas and a Happy New Year.

We wish you a Merry Christmas,
We wish you a Merry Christmas,
We wish you a Merry Christmas and a Happy New Year.
Good tidings we bring to you and your kin;
Good tidings for Christmas and a Happy New Year.

The First Noel

Text and music: Traditional English Carol, ca. 17th Century

The first Noel the angel did say
Was to certain poor shepherds in fields as they lay;

In fields as they lay, keeping their sheep,
On a cold winter's night that was so deep.
Noel, Noel, Noel, Noel,
Born is the King of Israel.

They looked up and saw a star
Shining in the east beyond them far,
And to the earth it gave great light,
And so it continued both day and night.
Noel, Noel, Noel, Noel,
Born is the King of Israel.

I Heard the Bells on Christmas Day

Text: Henry Wadsworth Longfellow, 1807–1882
Music: John Baptiste Calkin, 1827–1905

I heard the bells on Christmas Day
Their old familiar carols play.
And wild and sweet the words repeat
Of Peace on earth, good will to men.

I thought how as the day had come
The belfries of all Christendom
Had roll'd along th' unbroken song
Of Peace on earth, good will to men.

And in despair, I bow'd my head:
"There is no peace on earth," I said,
"For hate is strong and mocks the song,
Of Peace on earth, good will to men."

Then pealed the bells more loud and deep;
"God is not dead, nor doth He sleep;
The wrong shall fail, the right prevail,
With Peace on earth, good will to men."

Once in Royal David's City

Text: Cecil Francis Alexander, 1818–1895
Music: Henry J. Gauntlett, 1805–1876

Once in royal David's city,
Stood a lowly cattle shed,
Where a mother laid her Baby,
In a manger for His bed:
Mary was that mother mild,
Jesus Christ, her little Child.

He came down to earth from heaven,
Who is God and Lord of all,
And His shelter was a stable,
And His cradle was a stall:
With the poor, and mean, and lowly,
Lived on earth our Saviour holy.

For He is our childhood's pattern;
Day by day, like us, He grew;
He was little, weak, and helpless,
Tears and smiles, like us He knew;
And He cares when we are sad,
And he shares when we are glad.

And our eyes at last shall see Him,
Through His own redeeming love;
For that Child so dear and gentle,
Is our Lord in heaven above:
And He leads His children on,
To the place where He is gone.

While Shepherds Watched Their Flocks

Text: Nahum Tate, 1652–1715
Music: Yorkshire carol, ca. 1800

While shepherds watched
Their flocks by night

All seated on the ground
The angel of the Lord came down
And glory shone around
And glory shone around
"Fear not," said he,
For mighty dread
Had seized their troubled minds
"Glad tidings of great joy I bring
To you and all mankind,
To you and all mankind."

"To you in David's
Town this day
Is born of David's line
The Savior who is Christ the Lord
And this shall be the sign
And this shall be the sign."
"The heavenly Babe
You there shall find
To human view displayed
And meanly wrapped
In swathing bands
And in a manger laid
And in a manger laid."

Thus spake the seraph,
And forthwith
Appeared a shining throng
Of angels praising God, who thus
Addressed their joyful song
Addressed their joyful song
"All glory be to
God on high
And to the earth be peace;
Goodwill henceforth
From heaven to men
Begin and never cease
Begin and never cease!"

O Christmas Tree!

Traditional German Christmas Carol
Text and music: Anon.

O Christmas Tree! O Christmas Tree!
Thy leaves are so unchanging;
O Christmas Tree! O Christmas Tree!
Thy leaves are so unchanging;
Not only green when summer's here,
But also when 'tis cold and drear.
O Christmas Tree! O Christmas Tree!
Thy leaves are so unchanging!

O Christmas Tree! O Christmas Tree!
Much pleasure thou can'st give me;
O Christmas Tree! O Christmas Tree!
Much pleasure thou can'st give me;
How often has the Christmas tree
Afforded me the greatest glee!
O Christmas Tree! O Christmas Tree!
Much pleasure thou can'st give me.

O Christmas Tree! O Christmas Tree!
Thy candles shine so brightly!
O Christmas Tree! O Christmas Tree!
Thy candles shine so brightly!
From base to summit, gay and bright,
There's only splendor for the sight.
O Christmas Tree! O Christmas Tree!
Thy candles shine so brightly!

O Christmas Tree! O Christmas Tree!
How richly God has decked thee!
O Christmas Tree! O Christmas Tree!
How richly God has decked thee!
Thou bidst us true and faithful be,
And trust in God unchangingly.
O Christmas Tree! O Christmas Tree!
How richly God has decked thee!"

Deck the Halls with Boughs of Holly

Text: American, anon.
Music: Old Welsh melody, ca. 1600

Deck the halls with boughs of holly,
Fa la la la la, la la la la.
'Tis the season to be jolly,
Fa la la la la, la la la la.

Don we now our gay apparel,
Fa la la, la la la, la la la.
Troll the ancient Yule tide carol,
Fa la la la la, la la la la.

See the blazing Yule before us,
Fa la la la la, la la la la.
Strike the harp and join the chorus.
Fa la la la la, la la la la.

Follow me in merry measure,
Fa la la la la, la la la la.
While I tell of Yule tide treasure,
Fa la la la la, la la la la.

Fast away the old year passes,
Fa la la la la, la la la la.
Hail the new, ye lads and lasses,
Fa la la la la, la la la la.

Sing we joyous, all together,
Fa la la la la, la la la la.
Heedless of the wind and weather,
Fa la la la la, la la la la.

God Rest Ye Merry, Gentlemen

Traditional English Carol, ca. 1500

God rest ye merry, gentlemen
Let nothing you dismay
Remember, Christ, our Saviour

Was born on Christmas Day
To save us all from Satan's power
When we were gone astray
O tidings of comfort and joy,
Comfort and joy
O tidings of comfort and joy

In Bethlehem, in Israel,
This blessed Babe was born
And laid within a manger
Upon this blessed morn
The which His Mother Mary
Did nothing take in scorn
O tidings of comfort and joy,
Comfort and joy
O tidings of comfort and joy

From God our Heavenly Father
A blessed Angel came;
And unto certain Shepherds
Brought tidings of the same:
How that in Bethlehem was born
The Son of God by Name.
O tidings of comfort and joy,
Comfort and joy
O tidings of comfort and joy.

O Come, O Come, Emmanuel

Text: Latin, 12th Century
Translated from Latin to English by John M. Neale, 1851
Music: French origin, anon.

O come, O come, Emmanuel,
And ransom captive Israel,
That mourns in lonely exile here
Until the Son of God appear.
Rejoice! Rejoice!
Emmanuel shall come to thee, O Israel.

O come, thou Wisdom from on high,
Who orderest all things mightily;
To us the path of knowledge show,
And teach us in her ways to go.
Rejoice! Rejoice!
Emmanuel shall come to thee, O Israel.

O come, O come thou Lord of love
Declare thy law, all laws above
From captive exile bring release
And lead us in the way of peace.
Rejoice! Rejoice!
Emmanuel shall come to thee, O Israel.

O come, O come, great Lord of might,
Who to thy tribes on Sinai's height
In ancient times once gave the law
In cloud and majesty and awe.
Rejoice! Rejoice!
Emmanuel shall come to thee, O Israel

We Three Kings

Text and music: Rev. John Henry Hopkins, ca. 1857

We three kings of Orient are
Bearing gifts we traverse afar
Field and fountain, moor and mountain
Following yonder star
O Star of wonder, star of night
Star with royal beauty bright
Westward leading, still proceeding
Guide us to thy Perfect Light

Born a King on Bethlehem's plain
Gold I bring to crown Him again
King forever, ceasing never
Over us all to rein

O Star of wonder, star of night
Star with royal beauty bright
Westward leading, still proceeding
Guide us to Thy perfect light

O Holy Night

Text: Placide Cappeau de Roquemaure, ca. 1847
Translated from French to English by John Sullivan Dwight, 1812–1893
Music: Adolphe Charles Adams, 1803–1856

O holy night! The stars are brightly shining,
It is the night of our dear Saviour's birth.
Long lay the world in sin and error pining.
Till he appeared and the soul felt its worth.
A thrill of hope the weary world rejoices,
For yonder breaks a new and glorious morn.
Fall on your knees! Oh, hear the angel voices!
O night divine, O night when Christ was born;
O night, O holy night, O night divine!

Led by the light of faith serenely beaming,
With glowing hearts by His cradle we stand.
So led by light of a star sweetly gleaming,
Here came the wise men from out the Orient land.
The King of kings lay thus in lowly manger;
In all our trials born to be our friend.
He knows our need, to our weakness is no stranger,
Behold your King! Before him lowly bend!
Behold your King! Your king! Before him bend!

Truly He taught us to love one another,
His law is love and His gospel is peace.
Chains shall he break, for the slave is our brother.
And in his name all oppression shall cease.
Sweet hymns of joy in grateful chorus raise we,
Let all within us praise his holy name.
Christ is the Lord! Then ever, ever praise we,
His power and glory ever more proclaim!
His power and glory ever more proclaim!

Jingle Bells

James Lord Pierpont, ca. 1857

Dashing through the snow
On a one-horse open sleigh,
Over the fields we go,
Laughing all the way;
Bells on bob-tails ring,
Making spirits bright,
What fun it is to ride and sing
A sleighing song tonight
Jingle bells, jingle bells,
Jingle all the way!
O what fun it is to ride
In a one-horse open sleigh
Jingle bells, jingle bells,
Jingle all the way!
O what fun it is to ride
In a one-horse open sleigh

A day or two ago,
I thought I'd take a ride,
And soon Miss Fanny Bright
Was seated by my side.
The horse was lean and lank.
Misfortune seemed his lot.
He got into a drifted bank,
And we, we got upsot.
O, Jingle Bells, Jingle Bells,
Jingle all the way!
O what fun it is to ride
In a one-horse open sleigh.
Jingle bells, jingle bells,
Jingle all the way!
O what fun it is to ride
In a one-horse open sleigh.

The Twelve Days of Christmas

Traditional English Carol

On the first day of Christmas
My true love sent to me:
A partridge in a pear tree.

On the second day of Christmas
My true love sent to me:
Two turtle doves
And a partridge in a pear tree.

On the third day of Christmas
My true love sent to me:
Three French hens,
Two turtle doves
And a partridge in a pear tree.

On the fourth day of Christmas
My true love sent to me:
Four calling birds,
Three French hens,
Two turtle doves
And a partridge in a pear tree.

On the fifth day of Christmas
My true love sent to me:
Five golden rings,
Four calling birds,
Three French hens,
Two turtle doves
And a partridge in a pear tree.

On the sixth day of Christmas
My true love sent to me:
Six geese a laying,
Five golden rings,
Four calling birds,
Three French hens,

Two turtle doves
And a partridge in a pear tree.

On the seventh day of Christmas
My true love sent to me:
Seven swans a swimming,
Six geese a laying,
Five golden rings,
Four calling birds,
Three French hens,
Two turtle doves
And a partridge in a pear tree.

On the eighth day of Christmas
My true love sent to me:
Eight maids a milking,
Seven swans a swimming,
Six geese a laying,
Five golden rings,
Four calling birds,
Three French hens,
Two turtle doves
And a partridge in a pear tree.

On the ninth day of Christmas
My true love sent to me:
Nine ladies dancing,
Eight maids a milking,
Seven swans a swimming,
Six geese a laying,
Five golden rings,
Four calling birds,
Three French hens,
Two turtle doves
And a partridge in a pear tree.

On the tenth day of Christmas
My true love sent to me:
Ten lords a leaping,

Nine ladies dancing,
Eight maids a milking,
Seven swans a swimming,
Six geese a laying,
Five golden rings,
Four calling birds,
Three French hens,
Two turtle doves
And a partridge in a pear tree.

On the eleventh day of Christmas
My true love sent to me:
Eleven pipers piping,
Ten lords a leaping,
Nine ladies dancing,
Eight maids a milking,
Seven swans a swimming,
Six geese a laying,
Five golden rings,
Four calling birds,
Three French hens,
Two turtle doves
And a partridge in a pear tree.

On the twelfth day of Christmas
My true love sent to me:
Twelve drummers drumming,
Eleven pipers piping,
Ten lords a leaping,
Nine ladies dancing,
Eight maids a milking,
Seven swans a swimming,
Six geese a laying,
Five golden rings,
Four calling birds,
Three French hens,
Two turtle doves
And a partridge in a pear tree.

What Child Is This?

Text: William C. Dix, 1865.
Music: "Greensleeves," 16th Century English melody

What Child is this who, laid to rest
On Mary's lap is sleeping?
Whom angels greet with anthems sweet,
While shepherds watch are keeping?
This, this is Christ the King,
Whom shepherds guard and angels sing;
Haste, haste, to bring Him laud,
The Babe, the Son of Mary.

Why lies He in such mean estate,
Where ox and ass are feeding?
Good Christians, fear, for sinners here
The silent Word is pleading.
Nails, spear shall pierce Him through,
The cross be borne for me, for you.
Hail, hail the Word made flesh,
The Babe, the Son of Mary.

So bring Him incense, gold and myrrh,
Come peasant, king to own Him;
The King of kings salvation brings,
Let loving hearts enthrone Him.
Raise, raise a song on high,
The virgin sings her lullaby.
Joy, joy for Christ is born,
The Babe, the Son of Mary.

Far, Far Away on Judea's Plains

Text and Music: John Menzies Macfarlane, 1833–1892

Far, far away on Judea's plains,
Shepherds of old
Heard the joyous strains:

Chorus:
Glory to God, Glory to God,
Glory to God in the highest:
Peace on earth,
Good will to men;
Peace on earth,
Good will to men!

Sweet are these strains
Of redeeming love,
Message of mercy from heaven above:

Repeat Chorus

Lord, with the angels
We too would rejoice,
Help us to sing with the heart and voice:

Repeat Chorus

Hasten the time when,
From every clime,
Men shall unite
In the strains sublime:

Repeat Chorus

Index of Christmas Carols

Joy to the World 104
O, Come, All Ye Faithful 105
Angels We Have Heard on High 105
Silent Night 106
Away in a Manger 107
It Came upon the Midnight Clear 107
O Little Town of Bethlehem 108
Hark! The Herald Angels Sing 109
We Wish You a Merry Christmas 110
The First Noel 110
I Heard the Bells on Christmas Day 111
Once in Royal David's City 112

While Shepherds Watched
   Their Flocks 112
O Christmas Tree! 114
Deck the Halls with Boughs of Holly 115
God Rest Ye Merry, Gentlemen 115
O Come, O Come, Emmanuel 116
We Three Kings 117
O Holy Night 118
Jingle Bells 119
The Twelve Days of Christmas 120
What Child Is This? 123
Far, Far Away on Judea's Plains 123

Chapter Eleven
Fun and Games

C hristmas provides us with the perfect opportunity to relax and enjoy our family and friends. We should be having fun—not stressing out! At times it's nice to just sit and visit, but it's also nice to be able to set aside quality time for play. Games aren't just for children; they can be entertaining for everyone. This chapter is dedicated to having fun—without getting into trouble!

The Candy Cane Game (Spoons)

This game can be played using any kind of candy that can quickly be picked up. Candy canes work the best, but candy bars or any other packaged candy such as M&Ms®, Milk Duds, or malt balls will work. This game requires a deck of cards, so if you aren't comfortable using face cards, Rook, Skip-Bo, or Go Fish cards will work just as well.

The object of the game is to collect four cards of the same kind, such as four 2s, four 6s, or four 8s. Place the candy canes in the center of the table (with one candy cane fewer than the number of players) so that all the players can easily reach them. Each player is dealt four cards, and the remaining cards are placed face down in a deck near the dealer.

The dealer draws a card from the leftover deck and passes it, or one of the cards in his hand, face down to the person on his left. The player to the dealer's left takes the card and pulls one card from his hand (or the card he was just given) and passes it face down to the player on his left. Each player in turn does the same thing. All players should have four cards in their hand at all times. When the last player (seated on the right of the dealer) receives a card, he then discards it (or one of the cards in his hand) by placing it face down in a pile near the original deck. The dealer draws from this discarded pile once the original deck is used up.

The game continues until one player has four matching cards, at which time he quickly grabs a candy cane. The player who fails to grab a candy cane loses the round. If you want to keep score, players can be eliminated from the game once they can spell "candy canes" with their losses (or in other words have lost ten rounds). The last person remaining in the game is the winner and gets to keep the candy (and kindly share it with everyone else).

The Magic Elf Game

This game seems to stump even the brightest of participants, especially the young ones! Two people need to be in collaboration in preparation for this activity. The key to fooling everyone is for the collaborators to have a good secret code. This can be anything from knocking above a light switch (for a "no" answer) and below a light switch (for a "yes" answer) to scratching your head and pulling your earlobe.

At the beginning of the game, one of the two collaborators explains to everyone that his partner is one of Santa's elves. (If possible, have the partner dress like an elf.) Santa's elf is magic, and he knows everything that goes on in their home because he has elf friends who live in the walls. The first collaborator asks his elf partner to leave the room. Once the elf has left the room, his partner asks the other participants to choose (as a group) an item that has something to do with Christmas, such as a Christmas tree, a wreath, or the baby Jesus. When the group has made their decision, they call the elf back into the room without telling him what they chose. The partner asks the elf, "Is it a Christmas tree?" The elf knocks on the wall above the light switch, acts like he's listening to the wall, and answers, "No." (The first question asked should never be the correct answer.) The partner continues to question the elf with wrong answers, and the elf continues to knock above the light switch, listen to the wall, and answer, "No." Finally, when it's time to end the game, the elf knocks on the wall below the light switch, which signals to his partner that he is ready for the correct answer. The partner then asks, "Is it a wreath?" (or whatever the correct answer is), and the elf knocks on the wall (anywhere this time), listens, and answers, "Yes."

You don't have to use a light switch as your secret code, but you need to choose something subtle. You'll be surprised at how long it takes for someone to call your bluff!

Snow Fun—The Fox and the Hound

Christmas doesn't always bring snow, but it can be a lot of fun when it does. Another good Christmas activity is to bundle everyone up and go outside to play. You can teach the young ones to make snow angels, take them on a sleigh ride (with Dad or Mom pulling the sled), or help them build a snowman.

When I was young, the children in our neighborhood played a game called The Fox and the Hound. We made tracks in the snow to form a big circle and placed a mound of snow in the center of the circle that represented the hound's house (or what we referred to as the dog house). On the outer edge of the circle was another mound of snow for the fox's den. We added several more tracks from the edge of the circle leading to both the dog house and the fox's den.

The object of the game was to keep from getting caught by the hound. We couldn't leave the prepared tracks and go out into the fresh snow or we had to go to the dog house. If you could get to the fox's den when you were being chased, you were safe, but you could only stay there for sixty seconds. The hound could not stand in front of the den and wait for you to leave. During your sixty seconds of safety, he had to go chase someone else.

The hound would try to catch all the players and lock them in his house. You could free a friend if you could make it to the dog house, tag your friend, and get away before the hound could tag you. Once everyone was caught, the game was over.

Puzzles, Games, and Bingo

The following pages include word finds, a match game, crossword puzzles, a bingo game, and a couple of pictures that can be colored and cut apart to use as puzzles. Even big kids will enjoy these activities, especially if they participate in them with their children!

A Child Is Born

```
J  F  S  W  A  D  D  L  I  N  G  C  L  O  T  H  E  S  S  E  T  T  S  M  Y
F  C  I  P  B  D  D  K  D  M  N  U  E  L  O  V  E  P  K  S  H  M  A  C  S
R  D  L  E  L  U  A  W  B  K  Q  E  N  I  S  P  I  U  I  G  E  H  E  K  V
A  Y  H  I  L  W  I  S  E  M  E  N  W  A  D  H  L  T  I  H  B  H  C  5  V
N  Z  H  E  D  D  Z  Y  S  J  X  D  M  T  S  C  P  L  E  H  P  O  2  P  P
K  C  P  G  A  W  S  G  T  M  E  T  M  R  E  A  A  L  P  O  L  R  A  P  R
I  D  C  S  B  V  O  U  A  G  S  S  O  Y  B  S  H  M  R  F  E  C  N  T  K
N  O  D  T  V  R  E  P  R  I  A  W  U  E  R  T  T  P  E  B  S  G  I  S  B
C  N  M  R  F  B  O  N  R  M  R  B  H  S  E  R  S  A  M  L  S  K  M  A  M
E  K  Z  A  B  Z  M  H  L  W  A  T  R  B  C  Z  H  E  M  L  S  F  A  C  M
N  E  A  W  I  G  C  A  K  Y  N  T  W  I  F  H  C  F  E  E  J  J  L  R  H
S  Y  N  S  R  Y  F  G  N  H  F  F  T  I  E  E  R  P  W  D  N  Z  S  I  E
E  W  G  M  T  T  G  T  O  G  F  A  U  H  D  L  S  I  L  H  M  T  M  F  R
J  V  E  T  H  U  H  J  Z  I  E  H  T  B  E  O  J  O  S  E  P  H  W  I  O
B  F  L  V  D  L  U  A  I  P  W  R  E  H  G  W  G  I  M  T  R  C  S  C  D
V  Z  S  A  A  M  A  R  Y  A  P  E  A  C  E  O  N  E  A  R  T  H  G  E  C
B  O  R  N  Y  S  H  E  P  H  E  R  D  S  P  R  S  A  V  I  O  R  E  V  P
```

Angels
Animals
Bethlehem
Birthday
Born
Camels
Child
Christmas
December 25
Donkey
Fields
Flocks
Frankincense
Gabriel
Gold
Gospels

Hay
Heavenly Father
Herod
Jesus Christ
John the Baptist
Joseph
Light
Love
Luke
Manger
Mary
Matthew
Myrrh
New Testament
Peace on earth
Prophecy

Sacrifice
Savior
Shepherds
Star
Straw
Swaddling Clothes
Wise men
Worship

Answers on page 160

Here Comes Santa Claus

Word Find

```
L E L V E S C H R I S T M A S T R E E T R Y O S H
K P T I N S E L G A R L A N D W V V L S U S N E O
N E C Y N A K C H I L D R E N H E P G W D L D L L
Y A A C I N S S T O C K I N G S R N G R O E A V L
P C N R H T N O R N A M E N T S I M I E L I S M Y
O E D E K A O P O Q X A X V E T F B N A P G H I B
I O Y D R C W T S C O O K I E S C W G T H H E S E
N N C S E L M H Z S F I R E P L A C E H O N R T R
S E A U A A A W I N T E R W O N D E R L A N D L R
E A N I D U N G K S U G L I G H T S B T O Y S E I
T R E T M S R N E T S E U J T E X E R I R S W T E
T T W D W H U L T N O R T H P O L E E U C A B O S
I H S T N I C H O L A S F L Y E D I A Q H Y I E C
A P T E V I C S F C A R O L S F O N D N I C C N E
P R A S C X A E V E R G R E E N I R M A N G E L S
W E R I N E H Y M H R E I N D E E R A T G Z A J E
C B R X S P U D D I N G W D O L L S N C O M E T Z
```

Bicycle	Icicles	Pudding
Candy Cane	Lights	Red suit
Carols	Mistletoe	Reindeer
Children	North Pole	Rudolph
Christmas Tree	Ornaments	Santa Claus
Comet	Peace on earth	Seasons Greetings
Cookies	Poinsettia	Sleigh
Dasher		Snowman
Doll		St Nicholas
Elves		Star
Eve		Stockings
Evergreen		Tinsel
Fireplace		Toys
Garland		Train
Gingerbread man		Winter wonderland
Holly berries		Wreath

Answers on page 160

Merry Christmas

Word Find

```
T I A Q G M A G I Y B A B Y D O L L E B C L A M B
S E L C H R I S T M A S P L R S C G L I T T E R X
M T O Z K Y T D N Y N A D R E G K Y G S L E I G H
T S A W R E A T H Z F O A V A A S S B L I T Z E N
M P M R A A D V E N T P L D U N T O Y T R A I N U
A R G O O D I E S J Z E Y U L E C Z G D L L P Y C
R E C S L F D J W E S F Z J O Y P E I E Z G A Z A
Y J A F H A B K R A Y B E L L S D A R M C O A L R
C O N O N E P E T T Z O W W I S E M E N Q Z C Z O
H I D F R C P N T D E C K T H E H A L L S R J L L
R C Y M K Z A H L H P G R T W E N T Y F I F T H E
I E G C N S P N E J L Z S N O W G L O B E P K D R
S S P A R K L E D R T E F I G A N S I C O L D P S
T R P V H U B S Z L D O H B A B Y J E S U S H F V
I T S C R O O G E O E S G E C S T N I C K J Z J V
A A G G O S P E L C A R D S M T J Y S S T A B L E
N G I F T S P M K Y T I N Y T I M J O S E P H M F
```

Advent
Baby doll
Baby Jesus
Bells
Blitzen
Candle
Candy
Cards
Carolers
Christian
Christmas
Coal
Cold
Deck the halls
Gifts
Glitter
Goodies

Gospel
Joseph
Joy
Lamb
Magi
Mary
Prancer

Rejoice
Santas Elves
Scrooge
Shepherds
Sleigh
Snow Globe
Sparkle
St. Nick
Stable
Star of Bethlehem
Tiny Tim
Toy train
Twenty-fifth
Wise men
Wreath
Yule

Answers on page 160

130

Christmas Match Game

Copy the pictures twice, color them, cut them out, turn them face down, and try to match each object with its duplicate as you turn the pictures over.

Back side of Match Game cards

Christmas Match Game

Christmas Match Game

Christmas Match Game

Christmas Match Game

Christmas Magic Crossword Puzzle

Across

2. Merry Christmas and a _____ _____ _____
8. _____ old St. Nick
10. Whose birth do we celebrate on Christmas?
11. Santa wears _____ on his feet
12. Christmas _____
15. When does Santa come on Christmas Eve?
17. Rudolph was known for his _____ _____
19. A greeting at Christmastime
22. Meet me under the _____
23. How does Santa deliver his toys?
24. Another name for Santa
25. Merry _____

Down

1. Rudolph's nose _____
2. The _____ and the Ivy
3. Santa can't do it alone, so he has _____ to help him
4. In the song "The Twelve Days of Christmas," how many maids are milking?
5. Santa's beard and _____
6. Who loves Santa more than anyone else?
7. A red flower
9. _____ one another
13. In what month do some scholars believe that Jesus was born?
14. Santa has eight of these
16. Have you been _____ or nice?
18. If Santa can't come down the chimney, he comes through the _____ _____
20. Who proclaimed Christ's birth?
21. What makes Santa's reindeer fly?

Answers on page 160

Birth of Jesus   Crossword Puzzle

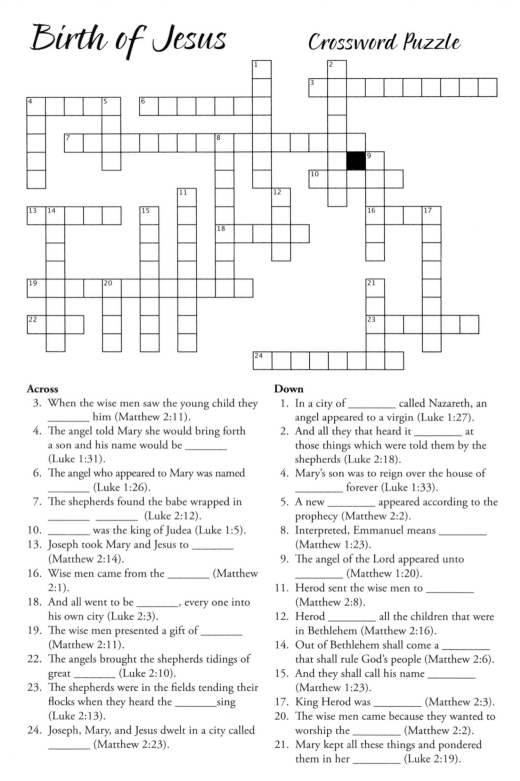

Across

3. When the wise men saw the young child they _____ him (Matthew 2:11).
4. The angel told Mary she would bring forth a son and his name would be _____ (Luke 1:31).
6. The angel who appeared to Mary was named _____ (Luke 1:26).
7. The shepherds found the babe wrapped in _____ _____ (Luke 2:12).
10. _____ was the king of Judea (Luke 1:5).
13. Joseph took Mary and Jesus to _____ (Matthew 2:14).
16. Wise men came from the _____ (Matthew 2:1).
18. And all went to be _____, every one into his own city (Luke 2:3).
19. The wise men presented a gift of _____ (Matthew 2:11).
22. The angels brought the shepherds tidings of great _____ (Luke 2:10).
23. The shepherds were in the fields tending their flocks when they heard the _____ sing (Luke 2:13).
24. Joseph, Mary, and Jesus dwelt in a city called _____ (Matthew 2:23).

Down

1. In a city of _____ called Nazareth, an angel appeared to a virgin (Luke 1:27).
2. And all they that heard it _____ at those things which were told them by the shepherds (Luke 2:18).
4. Mary's son was to reign over the house of _____ forever (Luke 1:33).
5. A new _____ appeared according to the prophecy (Matthew 2:2).
8. Interpreted, Emmanuel means _____ (Matthew 1:23).
9. The angel of the Lord appeared unto _____ (Matthew 1:20).
11. Herod sent the wise men to _____ (Matthew 2:8).
12. Herod _____ all the children that were in Bethlehem (Matthew 2:16).
14. Out of Bethlehem shall come a _____ that shall rule God's people (Matthew 2:6).
15. And they shall call his name _____ (Matthew 1:23).
17. King Herod was _____ (Matthew 2:3).
20. The wise men came because they wanted to worship the _____ (Matthew 2:2).
21. Mary kept all these things and pondered them in her _____ (Luke 2:19).

Answers on page 160

The Night Before Christmas
Crossword Puzzle

Across

5. The _____ before Christmas
8. Out on the _____
10. Mamma in her _____
11. He was dressed all in _____
12. The _____ were nestled all snug in their beds
13. No _____ were stirring
16. Up to the _____ the coursers they flew
19. When what to my wondering eyes should appear, but a miniature _____
20. His clothes were all _____
21. Visions of _____ danced in their heads
22. He shook when he _____
23. He called them by _____
24. His cheeks were like _____

Down

1. A _____ full of toys
2. More rapid than _____
3. Arose such a _____
4. _____ he exclaimed ere he drove out of sight
5. Just settled down for a long winter's _____
6. Dry leaves before the wild _____ fly
7. Stockings were hung by the _____
9. In hopes that _____ soon would be there
14. Down the chimney he came with a _____
15. A _____ of toys
17. He looked like a _____
18. I flew like a _____

Answers on page 160

Christmas Bingo

Materials

Verse cards (see below and on following page)
Medium-sized bowl
Bingo cards on pages 140–57

1 (1 lb.) pkg. small candy, such as M&Ms® or LifeSavers® (You can also use beans or buttons.)

Instructions

Choose one person to be the caller. Cut out the verse cards and put them in a medium-sized bowl. Cut out the Bingo cards and give one to each player. Have each player cover the free space (in the center of his Bingo card) with a small piece of candy, such as an M&M® or a Lifesaver®. (You can also use beans or buttons.)

The caller draws a card from the bowl and calls out the letter and verse on the card. The players check their Bingo cards (in the column under the letter that was called), and if the verse is on their card, they mark it with a piece of candy.

Diagonal Bingo

The caller continues to draw cards from the bowl and call out letters and verses until someone has a winning pattern on his Bingo card and yells "Bingo." (A winning pattern is a straight line of candy going horizontally, vertically, or diagonally—see photo with diagonal Bingo.) You can also play the game until someone has a blackout (or has covered his entire card with candy).

Verse cards

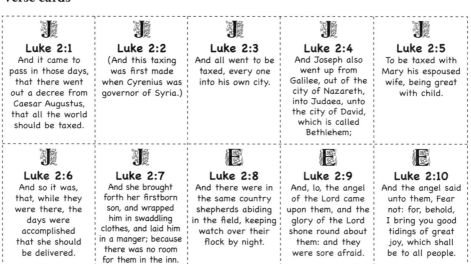

| **J** Luke 2:1 And it came to pass in those days, that there went out a decree from Caesar Augustus, that all the world should be taxed. | **J** Luke 2:2 (And this taxing was first made when Cyrenius was governor of Syria.) | **J** Luke 2:3 And all went to be taxed, every one into his own city. | **J** Luke 2:4 And Joseph also went up from Galilee, out of the city of Nazareth, into Judaea, unto the city of David, which is called Bethlehem; | **J** Luke 2:5 To be taxed with Mary his espoused wife, being great with child. |
| **J** Luke 2:6 And so it was, that, while they were there, the days were accomplished that she should be delivered. | **J** Luke 2:7 And she brought forth her firstborn son, and wrapped him in swaddling clothes, and laid him in a manger; because there was no room for them in the inn. | **E** Luke 2:8 And there were in the same country shepherds abiding in the field, keeping watch over their flock by night. | **E** Luke 2:9 And, lo, the angel of the Lord came upon them, and the glory of the Lord shone round about them: and they were sore afraid. | **E** Luke 2:10 And the angel said unto them, Fear not: for, behold, I bring you good tidings of great joy, which shall be to all people. |

Verse cards

Luke 2:11
For unto you is born this day in the city of David a Saviour, which is Christ the Lord.

Luke 2:12
And this shall be a sign unto you; Ye shall find the babe wrapped in swaddling clothes, lying in a manger.

Luke 2:13
And suddenly there was with the angel a multitude of the heavenly host praising God, and saying,

Luke 2:14
Glory to God in the highest, and on earth peace, good will toward men.

Luke 2:15
And...the shepherds said one to another, Let us now go even unto Bethlehem, and see this thing which is come to pass, which the Lord hath made known unto us.

Luke 2:16
And they came with haste, and found Mary, and Joseph, and the babe lying in a manger.

Luke 2:17
And when they had seen it, they made known abroad the saying which was told them concerning this child.

Luke 2:18
And all they that heard it wondered at those things which were told them by the shepherds.

Luke 2:19
But Mary kept all these things, and pondered them in her heart.

Luke 2:20
And the shepherds returned, glorifying and praising God for all the things that they had heard and seen, as it was told unto them.

Matthew 2:1
Now when Jesus was born in Bethlehem of Judaea in the days of Herod the king, behold, there came wise men from the east to Jerusalem,

Matthew 2:2
Saying, Where is he that is born King of the Jews? for we have seen his star in the east, and are come to worship him.

Matthew 2:3
When Herod the king had heard these things, he was troubled, and all Jerusalem with him.

Matthew 2:4
And when he had gathered all the chief priests and scribes of the people together, he demanded of them where Christ should be born.

Matthew 2:5
And they said unto him, In Bethlehem of Judaea: for thus it is written by the prophet,

Matthew 2:6
And thou Bethlehem, in the land of Juda, art not the least among the princes of Juda: for out of thee shall come a Governor, that shall rule my people Israel.

Matthew 2:7
Then Herod, when he had privily called the wise men, enquired of them diligently what time the star appeared.

Matthew 2:8
And he sent them to Bethlehem, and said, Go and search diligently for the young child; and when ye have found him, bring me word again, that I may come and worship him also.

Matthew 2:9
When they had heard the king, they departed; and, lo, the star, which they saw in the east, went before them, till it came and stood over where the young child was.

Matthew 2:10
When they saw the star, they rejoiced with exceeding great joy.

Matthew 2:11
And...they saw the young child with Mary his mother, and fell down, and worshipped him: and...they presented unto him gifts; gold, and frankincense, and myrrh.

Matthew 2:12
And being warned of God in a dream that they should not return to Herod, they departed into their own country another way.

Matthew 2:13
The angel of the Lord appeareth to Joseph in a dream, saying, Arise, and take the young child and his mother, and flee into Egypt.

Matthew 2:14
When he arose, he took the young child and his mother by night, and departed into Egypt:

Matthew 2:15
And was there until the death of Herod: that it might be fulfilled which was spoken of the Lord by the prophet, saying, Out of Egypt have I called my son.

Luke 2:2	Luke 2:9	Luke 2:20	Matthew 2:4	Matthew 2:11
(And this taxing was first made when Cyrenius was governor of Syria.)	And, lo, the angel of the Lord came upon them, and the glory of the Lord shone round about them: and they were sore afraid.	And the shepherds returned, glorifying and praising God for all the things that they had heard and seen, as it was told unto them.	And when he had gathered all the chief priests and scribes of the people together, he demanded of them where Christ should be born.	And...they saw the young child with Mary his mother, and fell down, and worshipped him: and...they presented unto him gifts; gold, and frankincense, and myrrh.
Luke 2:1	**Luke 2:12**	**Luke 2:16**	**Matthew 2:5**	**Matthew 2:9**
And it came to pass in those days, that there went out a decree from Caesar Augustus, that all the world should be taxed.	And this shall be a sign unto you; Ye shall find the babe wrapped in swaddling clothes, lying in a manger.	And they came with haste, and found Mary, and Joseph, and the babe lying in a manger.	And they said unto him, In Bethlehem of Judaea: for thus it is written by the prophet,	When they had heard the king, they departed; and, lo, the star, which they saw in the east, went before them, till it came and stood over where the young child was.
Luke 2:4	**Luke 2:10**	*Free Space*	**Matthew 2:3**	**Matthew 2:12**
And Joseph also went up from Galilee, out of the city of Nazareth, into Judaea, unto the city of David, which is called Bethlehem;	And the angel said unto them, Fear not: for, behold, I bring you good tidings of great joy, which shall be to all people.		When Herod the king had heard these things, he was troubled, and all Jerusalem with him.	And being warned of God in a dream that they should not return to Herod, they departed into their own country another way.
Luke 2:3	**Luke 2:8**	**Luke 2:18**	**Matthew 2:6**	**Matthew 2:15**
And all went to be taxed, every one into his own city.	And there were in the same country shepherds abiding in the field, keeping watch over their flock by night.	And all they that heard it wondered at those things which were told them by the shepherds.	And thou Bethlehem, in the land of Juda, art not the least among the princes of Juda: for out of thee shall come a Governor, that shall rule my people Israel.	And was there until the death of Herod: that it might be fulfilled which was spoken of the Lord by the prophet, saying, Out of Egypt have I called my son.
Luke 2:5	**Luke 2:11**	**Luke 2:15**	**Matthew 2:2**	**Matthew 2:10**
To be taxed with Mary his espoused wife, being great with child.	For unto you is born this day in the city of David a Saviour, which is Christ the Lord.	And...the shepherds said one to another, Let us now go even unto Bethlehem, and see this thing which is come to pass, which the Lord hath made known unto us.	Saying, Where is he that is born King of the Jews? for we have seen his star in the east, and are come to worship him.	When they saw the star, they rejoiced with exceeding great joy.

Christmas Bingo card 1

Luke 2:6	Luke 2:8	Luke 2:15	Matthew 2:3	Matthew 2:15
And so it was, that, while they were there, the days were accomplished that she should be delivered.	And there were in the same country shepherds abiding in the field, keeping watch over their flock by night.	And...the shepherds said one to another, Let us now go even unto Bethlehem, and see this thing which is come to pass, which the Lord hath made known unto us.	When Herod the king had heard these things, he was troubled, and all Jerusalem with him.	And was there until the death of Herod: that it might be fulfilled which was spoken of the Lord by the prophet, saying, Out of Egypt have I called my son.
Luke 2:7 And she brought forth her firstborn son, and wrapped him in swaddling clothes, and laid him in a manger; because there was no room for them in the inn.	**Luke 2:10** And the angel said unto them, Fear not: for, behold, I bring you good tidings of great joy, which shall be to all people.	**Luke 2:17** And when they had seen it, they made known abroad the saying which was told them concerning this child.	**Matthew 2:5** And they said unto him, In Bethlehem of Judaea: for thus it is written by the prophet,	**Matthew 2:13** The angel of the Lord appeareth to Joseph in a dream, saying, Arise, and take the young child and his mother, and flee into Egypt.
Luke 2:5 To be taxed with Mary his espoused wife, being great with child.	**Luke 2:12** And this shall be a sign unto you; Ye shall find the babe wrapped in swaddling clothes, lying in a manger.	*Free Space*	**Matthew 2:7** Then Herod, when he had privily called the wise men, enquired of them diligently what time the star appeared.	**Matthew 2:11** And...they saw the young child with Mary his mother, and fell down, and worshipped him: and...they presented unto him gifts; gold, and frankincense, and myrrh.
Luke 2:4 And Joseph also went up from Galilee, out of the city of Nazareth, into Judaea, unto the city of David, which is called Bethlehem;	**Luke 2:14** Glory to God in the highest, and on earth peace, good will toward men.	**Luke 2:19** But Mary kept all these things, and pondered them in her heart.	**Matthew 2:2** Saying, Where is he that is born King of the Jews? for we have seen his star in the east, and are come to worship him.	**Matthew 2:9** When they had heard the king, they departed; and, lo, the star, which they saw in the east, went before them, till it came and stood over where the young child was.
Luke 2:3 And all went to be taxed, every one into his own city.	**Luke 2:13** And suddenly there was with the angel a multitude of the heavenly host praising God, and saying,	**Matthew 2:1** Now when Jesus was born in Bethlehem of Judaea in the days of Herod the king, behold, there came wise men from the east to Jerusalem,	**Matthew 2:4** And when he had gathered all the chief priests and scribes of the people together, he demanded of them where Christ should be born.	**Matthew 2:14** When he arose, he took the young child and his mother by night, and departed into Egypt:

JESUS

Luke 2:7	Luke 2:9	Luke 2:16	Matthew 2:2	Matthew 2:14
And she brought forth her firstborn son, and wrapped him in swaddling clothes, and laid him in a manger; because there was no room for them in the inn.	And, lo, the angel of the Lord came upon them, and the glory of the Lord shone round about them: and they were sore afraid.	And they came with haste, and found Mary, and Joseph, and the babe lying in a manger.	Saying, Where is he that is born King of the Jews? for we have seen his star in the east, and are come to worship him.	When he arose, he took the young child and his mother by night, and departed into Egypt:
Luke 2:5	**Luke 2:11**	**Luke 2:18**	**Matthew 2:4**	**Matthew 2:12**
To be taxed with Mary his espoused wife, being great with child.	For unto you is born this day in the city of David a Saviour, which is Christ the Lord.	And all they that heard it wondered at those things which were told them by the shepherds.	And when he had gathered all the chief priests and scribes of the people together, he demanded of them where Christ should be born.	And being warned of God in a dream that they should not return to Herod, they departed into their own country another way.
Luke 2:3	**Luke 2:13**		**Matthew 2:6**	**Matthew 2:10**
And all went to be taxed, every one into his own city.	And suddenly there was with the angel a multitude of the heavenly host praising God, and saying,	*Free Space*	And thou Bethlehem, in the land of Juda, art not the least among the princes of Juda: for out of thee shall come a Governor, that shall rule my people Israel.	When they saw the star, they rejoiced with exceeding great joy.
Luke 2:1	**Luke 2:8**	**Luke 2:20**	**Matthew 2:8**	**Matthew 2:15**
And it came to pass in those days, that there went out a decree from Caesar Augustus, that all the world should be taxed.	And there were in the same country shepherds abiding in the field, keeping watch over their flock by night.	And the shepherds returned, glorifying and praising God for all the things that they had heard and seen, as it was told unto them.	And he sent them to Bethlehem, and said, Go and search diligently for the young child; and when ye have found him, bring me word again, that I may come and worship him also.	And was there until the death of Herod: that it might be fulfilled which was spoken of the Lord by the prophet, saying, Out of Egypt have I called my son.
Luke 2:2	**Luke 2:14**	**Luke 2:15**	**Matthew 2:3**	**Matthew 2:9**
(And this taxing was first made when Cyrenius was governor of Syria.)	Glory to God in the highest, and on earth peace, good will toward men.	And...the shepherds said one to another, Let us now go even unto Bethlehem, and see this thing which is come to pass, which the Lord hath made known unto us.	When Herod the king had heard these things, he was troubled, and all Jerusalem with him.	When they had heard the king, they departed; and, lo, the star, which they saw in the east, went before them, till it came and stood over where the young child was.

Christmas Bingo card 3

JESUS

Luke 2:1	Luke 2:14	Luke 2:18	Matthew 2:4	Matthew 2:9
And it came to pass in those days, that there went out a decree from Caesar Augustus, that all the world should be taxed.	Glory to God in the highest, and on earth peace, good will toward men.	And all they that heard it wondered at those things which were told them by the shepherds.	And when he had gathered all the chief priests and scribes of the people together, he demanded of them where Christ should be born.	When they had heard the king, they departed; and, lo, the star, which they saw in the east, went before them, till it came and stood over where the young child was.
Luke 2:3	**Luke 2:11**	**Luke 2:17**	**Matthew 2:7**	**Matthew 2:11**
And all went to be taxed, every one into his own city.	For unto you is born this day in the city of David a Saviour, which is Christ the Lord.	And when they had seen it, they made known abroad the saying which was told them concerning this child.	Then Herod, when he had privily called the wise men, enquired of them diligently what time the star appeared.	And...they saw the young child with Mary his mother, and fell down, and worshipped him: and...they presented unto him gifts; gold, and frankincense, and myrrh.
Luke 2:5	**Luke 2:8**	 *Free Space*	**Matthew 2:2**	**Matthew 2:13**
To be taxed with Mary his espoused wife, being great with child.	And there were in the same country shepherds abiding in the field, keeping watch over their flock by night.		Saying, Where is he that is born King of the Jews? for we have seen his star in the east, and are come to worship him.	The angel of the Lord appeareth to Joseph in a dream, saying, Arise, and take the young child and his mother, and flee into Egypt.
Luke 2:7	**Luke 2:9**	**Luke 2:20**	**Matthew 2:5**	**Matthew 2:15**
And she brought forth her firstborn son, and wrapped him in swaddling clothes, and laid him in a manger; because there was no room for them in the inn.	And, lo, the angel of the Lord came upon them, and the glory of the Lord shone round about them: and they were sore afraid.	And the shepherds returned, glorifying and praising God for all the things that they had heard and seen, as it was told unto them.	And they said unto him, In Bethlehem of Judaea: for thus it is written by the prophet,	And was there until the death of Herod: that it might be fulfilled which was spoken of the Lord by the prophet, saying, Out of Egypt have I called my son.
Luke 2:6	**Luke 2:12**	**Luke 2:19**	**Matthew 2:8**	**Matthew 2:10**
And so it was, that, while they were there, the days were accomplished that she should be delivered.	And this shall be a sign unto you; Ye shall find the babe wrapped in swaddling clothes, lying in a manger.	But Mary kept all these things, and pondered them in her heart.	And he sent them to Bethlehem, and said, Go and search diligently for the young child; and when ye have found him, bring me word again, that I may come and worship him also.	When they saw the star, they rejoiced with exceeding great joy.

JESUS

Luke 2:3	**Luke 2:12**	**Matthew 2:1**	**Matthew 2:7**	**Matthew 2:14**
And all went to be taxed, every one into his own city.	And this shall be a sign unto you; Ye shall find the babe wrapped in swaddling clothes, lying in a manger.	Now when Jesus was born in Bethlehem of Judaea in the days of Herod the king, behold, there came wise men from the east to Jerusalem,	Then Herod, when he had privily called the wise men, enquired of them diligently what time the star appeared.	When he arose, he took the young child and his mother by night, and departed into Egypt:
Luke 2:5	**Luke 2:13**	**Luke 2:19**	**Matthew 2:6**	**Matthew 2:12**
To be taxed with Mary his espoused wife, being great with child.	And suddenly there was with the angel a multitude of the heavenly host praising God, and saying,	But Mary kept all these things, and pondered them in her heart.	And thou Bethlehem, in the land of Juda, art not the least among the princes of Juda: for out of thee shall come a Governor, that shall rule my people Israel.	And being warned of God in a dream that they should not return to Herod, they departed into their own country another way.
Luke 2:6	**Luke 2:8**	*Free Space* 	**Matthew 2:4**	**Matthew 2:9**
And so it was, that, while they were there, the days were accomplished that she should be delivered.	And there were in the same country shepherds abiding in the field, keeping watch over their flock by night.		And when he had gathered all the chief priests and scribes of the people together, he demanded of them where Christ should be born.	When they had heard the king, they departed; and, lo, the star, which they saw in the east, went before them, till it came and stood over where the young child was.
Luke 2:4	**Luke 2:9**	**Luke 2:17**	**Matthew 2:3**	**Matthew 2:15**
And Joseph also went up from Galilee, out of the city of Nazareth, into Judaea, unto the city of David, which is called Bethlehem;	And, lo, the angel of the Lord came upon them, and the glory of the Lord shone round about them: and they were sore afraid.	And when they had seen it, they made known abroad the saying which was told them concerning this child.	When Herod the king had heard these things, he was troubled, and all Jerusalem with him.	And was there until the death of Herod: that it might be fulfilled which was spoken of the Lord by the prophet, saying, Out of Egypt have I called my son.
Luke 2:2	**Luke 2:10**	**Luke 2:15**	**Matthew 2:5**	**Matthew 2:11**
(And this taxing was first made when Cyrenius was governor of Syria.)	And the angel said unto them, Fear not: for, behold, I bring you good tidings of great joy, which shall be to all people.	And...the shepherds said one to another, Let us now go even unto Bethlehem, and see this thing which is come to pass, which the Lord hath made known unto us.	And they said unto him, In Bethlehem of Judaea: for thus it is written by the prophet,	And...they saw the young child with Mary his mother, and fell down, and worshipped him: and...they presented unto him gifts; gold, and frankincense, and myrrh.

Christmas Bingo card 5

JESUS

Luke 2:2	Luke 2:13	Matthew 2:1	Matthew 2:7	Matthew 2:10
(And this taxing was first made when Cyrenius was governor of Syria.)	And suddenly there was with the angel a multitude of the heavenly host praising God, and saying,	Now when Jesus was born in Bethlehem of Judaea in the days of Herod the king, behold, there came wise men from the east to Jerusalem,	Then Herod, when he had privily called the wise men, enquired of them diligently what time the star appeared.	When they saw the star, they rejoiced with exceeding great joy.
Luke 2:5	**Luke 2:12**	**Luke 2:15**	**Matthew 2:4**	**Matthew 2:12**
To be taxed with Mary his espoused wife, being great with child.	And this shall be a sign unto you; Ye shall find the babe wrapped in swaddling clothes, lying in a manger.	And...the shepherds said one to another, Let us now go even unto Bethlehem, and see this thing which is come to pass, which the Lord hath made known unto us.	And when he had gathered all the chief priests and scribes of the people together, he demanded of them where Christ should be born.	And being warned of God in a dream that they should not return to Herod, they departed into their own country another way.
Luke 2:1	**Luke 2:14**	 *Free Space*	**Matthew 2:2**	**Matthew 2:14**
And it came to pass in those days, that there went out a decree from Caesar Augustus, that all the world should be taxed.	Glory to God in the highest, and on earth peace, good will toward men.		Saying, Where is he that is born King of the Jews? for we have seen his star in the east, and are come to worship him.	When he arose, he took the young child and his mother by night, and departed into Egypt:
Luke 2:4	**Luke 2:9**	**Luke 2:20**	**Matthew 2:5**	**Matthew 2:15**
And Joseph also went up from Galilee, out of the city of Nazareth, into Judaea, unto the city of David, which is called Bethlehem;	And, lo, the angel of the Lord came upon them, and the glory of the Lord shone round about them: and they were sore afraid.	And the shepherds returned, glorifying and praising God for all the things that they had heard and seen, as it was told unto them.	And they said unto him, In Bethlehem of Judaea: for thus it is written by the prophet,	And was there until the death of Herod: that it might be fulfilled which was spoken of the Lord by the prophet, saying, Out of Egypt have I called my son.
Luke 2:7	**Luke 2:10**	**Luke 2:16**	**Matthew 2:8**	**Matthew 2:9**
And she brought forth her firstborn son, and wrapped him in swaddling clothes, and laid him in a manger; because there was no room for them in the inn.	And the angel said unto them, Fear not: for, behold, I bring you good tidings of great joy, which shall be to all people.	And they came with haste, and found Mary, and Joseph, and the babe lying in a manger.	And he sent them to Bethlehem, and said, Go and search diligently for the young child; and when ye have found him, bring me word again, that I may come and worship him also.	When they had heard the king, they departed; and, lo, the star, which they saw in the east, went before them, till it came and stood over where the young child was.

JESUS

Luke 2:3	**Luke 2:8**	**Luke 2:20**	**Matthew 2:2**	**Matthew 2:13**
And all went to be taxed, every one into his own city.	And there were in the same country shepherds abiding in the field, keeping watch over their flock by night.	And the shepherds returned, glorifying and praising God for all the things that they had heard and seen, as it was told unto them.	Saying, Where is he that is born King of the Jews? for we have seen his star in the east, and are come to worship him.	The angel of the Lord appeareth to Joseph in a dream, saying, Arise, and take the young child and his mother, and flee into Egypt.
Luke 2:1	**Luke 2:9**	**Luke 2:16**	**Matthew 2:5**	**Matthew 2:15**
And it came to pass in those days, that there went out a decree from Caesar Augustus, that all the world should be taxed.	And, lo, the angel of the Lord came upon them, and the glory of the Lord shone round about them: and they were sore afraid.	And they came with haste, and found Mary, and Joseph, and the babe lying in a manger.	And they said unto him, In Bethlehem of Judaea: for thus it is written by the prophet,	And was there until the death of Herod: that it might be fulfilled which was spoken of the Lord by the prophet, saying, Out of Egypt have I called my son.
Luke 2:6	**Luke 2:10**	*Free Space*	**Matthew 2:8**	**Matthew 2:11**
And so it was, that, while they were there, the days were accomplished that she should be delivered.	And the angel said unto them, Fear not: for, behold, I bring you good tidings of great joy, which shall be to all people.		And he sent them to Bethlehem, and said, Go and search diligently for the young child; and when ye have found him, bring me word again, that I may come and worship him also.	And...they saw the young child with Mary his mother, and fell down, and worshipped him: and...they presented unto him gifts; gold, and frankincense, and myrrh.
Luke 2:4	**Luke 2:11**	**Luke 2:19**	**Matthew 2:3**	**Matthew 2:12**
And Joseph also went up from Galilee, out of the city of Nazareth, into Judaea, unto the city of David, which is called Bethlehem;	For unto you is born this day in the city of David a Saviour, which is Christ the Lord.	But Mary kept all these things, and pondered them in her heart.	When Herod the king had heard these things, he was troubled, and all Jerusalem with him.	And being warned of God in a dream that they should not return to Herod, they departed into their own country another way.
Luke 2:5	**Luke 2:12**	**Luke 2:17**	**Matthew 2:7**	**Matthew 2:14**
To be taxed with Mary his espoused wife, being great with child.	And this shall be a sign unto you; Ye shall find the babe wrapped in swaddling clothes, lying in a manger.	And when they had seen it, they made known abroad the saying which was told them concerning this child.	Then Herod, when he had privily called the wise men, enquired of them diligently what time the star appeared.	When he arose, he took the young child and his mother by night, and departed into Egypt:

Christmas Bingo card 7

Luke 2:7	Luke 2:13	Luke 2:18	Matthew 2:4	Matthew 2:10
And she brought forth her firstborn son, and wrapped him in swaddling clothes, and laid him in a manger; because there was no room for them in the inn.	And suddenly there was with the angel a multitude of the heavenly host praising God, and saying,	And all they that heard it wondered at those things which were told them by the shepherds.	And when he had gathered all the chief priests and scribes of the people together, he demanded of them where Christ should be born.	When they saw the star, they rejoiced with exceeding great joy.
Luke 2:5 To be taxed with Mary his espoused wife, being great with child.	**Luke 2:14** Glory to God in the highest, and on earth peace, good will toward men.	**Luke 2:17** And when they had seen it, they made known abroad the saying which was told them concerning this child.	**Matthew 2:6** And thou Bethlehem, in the land of Juda, art not the least among the princes of Juda: for out of thee shall come a Governor, that shall rule my people Israel.	**Matthew 2:15** And was there until the death of Herod: that it might be fulfilled which was spoken of the Lord by the prophet, saying, Out of Egypt have I called my son.
Luke 2:3 And all went to be taxed, every one into his own city.	**Luke 2:11** For unto you is born this day in the city of David a Saviour, which is Christ the Lord.	 *Free Space*	**Matthew 2:2** Saying, Where is he that is born King of the Jews? for we have seen his star in the east, and are come to worship him.	**Matthew 2:14** When he arose, he took the young child and his mother by night, and departed into Egypt:
Luke 2:1 And it came to pass in those days, that there went out a decree from Caesar Augustus, that all the world should be taxed.	**Luke 2:10** And the angel said unto them, Fear not: for, behold, I bring you good tidings of great joy, which shall be to all people.	**Luke 2:19** But Mary kept all these things, and pondered them in her heart.	**Matthew 2:5** And they said unto him, In Bethlehem of Judaea: for thus it is written by the prophet,	**Matthew 2:13** The angel of the Lord appeareth to Joseph in a dream, saying, Arise, and take the young child and his mother, and flee into Egypt.
Luke 2:6 And so it was, that, while they were there, the days were accomplished that she should be delivered.	**Luke 2:9** And, lo, the angel of the Lord came upon them, and the glory of the Lord shone round about them: and they were sore afraid.	**Luke 2:16** And they came with haste, and found Mary, and Joseph, and the babe lying in a manger.	**Matthew 2:3** When Herod the king had heard these things, he was troubled, and all Jerusalem with him.	**Matthew 2:12** And being warned of God in a dream that they should not return to Herod, they departed into their own country another way.

JESUS

Luke 2:4 And Joseph also went up from Galilee, out of the city of Nazareth, into Judaea, unto the city of David, which is called Bethlehem;	**Luke 2:8** And there were in the same country shepherds abiding in the field, keeping watch over their flock by night.	**Matthew 2:1** Now when Jesus was born in Bethlehem of Judaea in the days of Herod the king, behold, there came wise men from the east to Jerusalem,	**Matthew 2:8** And he sent them to Bethlehem, and said, Go and search diligently for the young child; and when ye have found him, bring me word again, that I may come and worship him also.	**Matthew 2:12** And being warned of God in a dream that they should not return to Herod, they departed into their own country another way.
Luke 2:2 (And this taxing was first made when Cyrenius was governor of Syria.)	**Luke 2:14** Glory to God in the highest, and on earth peace, good will toward men.	**Luke 2:15** And...the shepherds said one to another, Let us now go even unto Bethlehem, and see this thing which is come to pass, which the Lord hath made known unto us.	**Matthew 2:7** Then Herod, when he had privily called the wise men, enquired of them diligently what time the star appeared.	**Matthew 2:10** When they saw the star, they rejoiced with exceeding great joy.
Luke 2:1 And it came to pass in those days, that there went out a decree from Caesar Augustus, that all the world should be taxed.	**Luke 2:9** And, lo, the angel of the Lord came upon them, and the glory of the Lord shone round about them: and they were sore afraid.	 *Free Space*	**Matthew 2:6** And thou Bethlehem, in the land of Juda, art not the least among the princes of Juda: for out of thee shall come a Governor, that shall rule my people Israel.	**Matthew 2:15** And was there until the death of Herod: that it might be fulfilled which was spoken of the Lord by the prophet, saying, Out of Egypt have I called my son.
Luke 2:3 And all went to be taxed, every one into his own city.	**Luke 2:13** And suddenly there was with the angel a multitude of the heavenly host praising God, and saying,	**Luke 2:19** But Mary kept all these things, and pondered them in her heart.	**Matthew 2:3** When Herod the king had heard these things, he was troubled, and all Jerusalem with him.	**Matthew 2:13** The angel of the Lord appeareth to Joseph in a dream, saying, Arise, and take the young child and his mother, and flee into Egypt.
Luke 2:5 To be taxed with Mary his espoused wife, being great with child.	**Luke 2:11** For unto you is born this day in the city of David a Saviour, which is Christ the Lord.	**Luke 2:17** And when they had seen it, they made known abroad the saying which was told them concerning this child.	**Matthew 2:2** Saying, Where is he that is born King of the Jews? for we have seen his star in the east, and are come to worship him.	**Matthew 2:9** When they had heard the king, they departed; and, lo, the star, which they saw in the east, went before them, till it came and stood over where the young child was.

Christmas Bingo card 9

Luke 2:5	Luke 2:12	Luke 2:15	Matthew 2:3	Matthew 2:10
To be taxed with Mary his espoused wife, being great with child.	And this shall be a sign unto you; Ye shall find the babe wrapped in swaddling clothes, lying in a manger.	And...the shepherds said one to another, Let us now go even unto Bethlehem, and see this thing which is come to pass, which the Lord hath made known unto us.	When Herod the king had heard these things, he was troubled, and all Jerusalem with him.	When they saw the star, they rejoiced with exceeding great joy.
Luke 2:2 (And this taxing was first made when Cyrenius was governor of Syria.)	**Luke 2:8** And there were in the same country shepherds abiding in the field, keeping watch over their flock by night.	**Luke 2:16** And they came with haste, and found Mary, and Joseph, and the babe lying in a manger.	**Matthew 2:5** And they said unto him, In Bethlehem of Judaea: for thus it is written by the prophet,	**Matthew 2:9** When they had heard the king, they departed; and, lo, the star, which they saw in the east, went before them, till it came and stood over where the young child was.
Luke 2:4 And Joseph also went up from Galilee, out of the city of Nazareth, into Judaea, unto the city of David, which is called Bethlehem;	**Luke 2:13** And suddenly there was with the angel a multitude of the heavenly host praising God, and saying,	 *Free Space*	**Matthew 2:7** Then Herod, when he had privily called the wise men, enquired of them diligently what time the star appeared.	**Matthew 2:12** And being warned of God in a dream that they should not return to Herod, they departed into their own country another way.
Luke 2:1 And it came to pass in those days, that there went out a decree from Caesar Augustus, that all the world should be taxed.	**Luke 2:11** For unto you is born this day in the city of David a Saviour, which is Christ the Lord.	**Luke 2:17** And when they had seen it, they made known abroad the saying which was told them concerning this child.	**Matthew 2:8** And he sent them to Bethlehem, and said, Go and search diligently for the young child; and when ye have found him, bring me word again, that I may come and worship him also.	**Matthew 2:11** And...they saw the young child with Mary his mother, and fell down, and worshipped him: and...they presented unto him gifts; gold, and frankincense, and myrrh.
Luke 2:3 And all went to be taxed, every one into his own city.	**Luke 2:10** And the angel said unto them, Fear not: for, behold, I bring you good tidings of great joy, which shall be to all people.	**Luke 2:18** And all they that heard it wondered at those things which were told them by the shepherds.	**Matthew 2:2** Saying, Where is he that is born King of the Jews? for we have seen his star in the east, and are come to worship him.	**Matthew 2:14** When he arose, he took the young child and his mother by night, and departed into Egypt:

JESUS

Luke 2:7	Luke 2:14	Luke 2:19	Matthew 2:6	Matthew 2:11
And she brought forth her firstborn son, and wrapped him in swaddling clothes, and laid him in a manger; because there was no room for them in the inn.	Glory to God in the highest, and on earth peace, good will toward men.	But Mary kept all these things, and pondered them in her heart.	And thou Bethlehem, in the land of Juda, art not the least among the princes of Juda: for out of thee shall come a Governor, that shall rule my people Israel.	And...they saw the young child with Mary his mother, and fell down, and worshipped him: and...they presented unto him gifts; gold, and frankincense, and myrrh.
Luke 2:4	**Luke 2:12**	**Luke 2:16**	**Matthew 2:4**	**Matthew 2:9**
And Joseph also went up from Galilee, out of the city of Nazareth, into Judaea, unto the city of David, which is called Bethlehem;	And this shall be a sign unto you; Ye shall find the babe wrapped in swaddling clothes, lying in a manger.	And they came with haste, and found Mary, and Joseph, and the babe lying in a manger.	And when he had gathered all the chief priests and scribes of the people together, he demanded of them where Christ should be born.	When they had heard the king, they departed; and, lo, the star, which they saw in the east, went before them, till it came and stood over where the young child was.
Luke 2:6	**Luke 2:9**	Free Space	**Matthew 2:8**	**Matthew 2:14**
And so it was, that, while they were there, the days were accomplished that she should be delivered.	And, lo, the angel of the Lord came upon them, and the glory of the Lord shone round about them: and they were sore afraid.		And he sent them to Bethlehem, and said, Go and search diligently for the young child; and when ye have found him, bring me word again, that I may come and worship him also.	When he arose, he took the young child and his mother by night, and departed into Egypt:
Luke 2:3	**Luke 2:13**	**Luke 2:15**	**Matthew 2:3**	**Matthew 2:15**
And all went to be taxed, every one into his own city.	And suddenly there was with the angel a multitude of the heavenly host praising God, and saying,	And...the shepherds said one to another, Let us now go even unto Bethlehem, and see this thing which is come to pass, which the Lord hath made known unto us.	When Herod the king had heard these things, he was troubled, and all Jerusalem with him.	And was there until the death of Herod: that it might be fulfilled which was spoken of the Lord by the prophet, saying, Out of Egypt have I called my son.
Luke 2:5	**Luke 2:11**	**Matthew 2:1**	**Matthew 2:5**	**Matthew 2:10**
To be taxed with Mary his espoused wife, being great with child.	For unto you is born this day in the city of David a Saviour, which is Christ the Lord.	Now when Jesus was born in Bethlehem of Judaea in the days of Herod the king, behold, there came wise men from the east to Jerusalem,	And they said unto him, In Bethlehem of Judaea: for thus it is written by the prophet,	When they saw the star, they rejoiced with exceeding great joy.

Christmas Bingo card 11

JESUS

Luke 2:1	Luke 2:9	Luke 2:18	Matthew 2:2	Matthew 2:15
And it came to pass in those days, that there went out a decree from Caesar Augustus, that all the world should be taxed.	And, lo, the angel of the Lord came upon them, and the glory of the Lord shone round about them: and they were sore afraid.	And all they that heard it wondered at those things which were told them by the shepherds.	Saying, Where is he that is born King of the Jews? for we have seen his star in the east, and are come to worship him.	And was there until the death of Herod: that it might be fulfilled which was spoken of the Lord by the prophet, saying, Out of Egypt have I called my son.
Luke 2:4	**Luke 2:11**	**Luke 2:17**	**Matthew 2:5**	**Matthew 2:11**
And Joseph also went up from Galilee, out of the city of Nazareth, into Judaea, unto the city of David, which is called Bethlehem;	For unto you is born this day in the city of David a Saviour, which is Christ the Lord.	And when they had seen it, they made known abroad the saying which was told them concerning this child.	And they said unto him, In Bethlehem of Judaea: for thus it is written by the prophet,	And...they saw the young child with Mary his mother, and fell down, and worshipped him: and...they presented unto him gifts; gold, and frankincense, and myrrh.
Luke 2:2	**Luke 2:14**	*Free Space*	**Matthew 2:6**	**Matthew 2:13**
(And this taxing was first made when Cyrenius was governor of Syria.)	Glory to God in the highest, and on earth peace, good will toward men.		And thou Bethlehem, in the land of Juda, art not the least among the princes of Juda: for out of thee shall come a Governor, that shall rule my people Israel.	The angel of the Lord appeareth to Joseph in a dream, saying, Arise, and take the young child and his mother, and flee into Egypt.
Luke 2:5	**Luke 2:13**	**Luke 2:19**	**Matthew 2:4**	**Matthew 2:10**
To be taxed with Mary his espoused wife, being great with child.	And suddenly there was with the angel a multitude of the heavenly host praising God, and saying,	But Mary kept all these things, and pondered them in her heart.	And when he had gathered all the chief priests and scribes of the people together, he demanded of them where Christ should be born.	When they saw the star, they rejoiced with exceeding great joy.
Luke 2:3	**Luke 2:10**	**Luke 2:16**	**Matthew 2:3**	**Matthew 2:9**
And all went to be taxed, every one into his own city.	And the angel said unto them, Fear not: for, behold, I bring you good tidings of great joy, which shall be to all people.	And they came with haste, and found Mary, and Joseph, and the babe lying in a manger.	When Herod the king had heard these things, he was troubled, and all Jerusalem with him.	When they had heard the king, they departed; and, lo, the star, which they saw in the east, went before them, till it came and stood over where the young child was.

Luke 2:3	Luke 2:12	Luke 2:20	Matthew 2:7	Matthew 2:13
And all went to be taxed, every one into his own city.	And this shall be a sign unto you; Ye shall find the babe wrapped in swaddling clothes, lying in a manger.	And the shepherds returned, glorifying and praising God for all the things that they had heard and seen, as it was told unto them.	Then Herod, when he had privily called the wise men, enquired of them diligently what time the star appeared.	The angel of the Lord appeareth to Joseph in a dream, saying, Arise, and take the young child and his mother, and flee into Egypt.
Luke 2:7 And she brought forth her firstborn son, and wrapped him in swaddling clothes, and laid him in a manger; because there was no room for them in the inn.	**Luke 2:13** And suddenly there was with the angel a multitude of the heavenly host praising God, and saying,	**Matthew 2:1** Now when Jesus was born in Bethlehem of Judaea in the days of Herod the king, behold, there came wise men from the east to Jerusalem,	**Matthew 2:8** And he sent them to Bethlehem, and said, Go and search diligently for the young child; and when ye have found him, bring me word again, that I may come and worship him also.	**Matthew 2:10** When they saw the star, they rejoiced with exceeding great joy.
Luke 2:1 And it came to pass in those days, that there went out a decree from Caesar Augustus, that all the world should be taxed.	**Luke 2:10** And the angel said unto them, Fear not: for, behold, I bring you good tidings of great joy, which shall be to all people.	*Free Space*	**Matthew 2:5** And they said unto him, In Bethlehem of Judaea: for thus it is written by the prophet,	**Matthew 2:15** And was there until the death of Herod: that it might be fulfilled which was spoken of the Lord by the prophet, saying, Out of Egypt have I called my son.
Luke 2:4 And Joseph also went up from Galilee, out of the city of Nazareth, into Judaea, unto the city of David, which is called Bethlehem;	**Luke 2:11** For unto you is born this day in the city of David a Saviour, which is Christ the Lord.	**Luke 2:17** And when they had seen it, they made known abroad the saying which was told them concerning this child.	**Matthew 2:6** And thou Bethlehem, in the land of Juda, art not the least among the princes of Juda: for out of thee shall come a Governor, that shall rule my people Israel.	**Matthew 2:14** When he arose, he took the young child and his mother by night, and departed into Egypt:
Luke 2:6 And so it was, that, while they were there, the days were accomplished that she should be delivered.	**Luke 2:9** And, lo, the angel of the Lord came upon them, and the glory of the Lord shone round about them: and they were sore afraid.	**Luke 2:15** And...the shepherds said one to another, Let us now go even unto Bethlehem, and see this thing which is come to pass, which the Lord hath made known unto us.	**Matthew 2:3** When Herod the king had heard these things, he was troubled, and all Jerusalem with him.	**Matthew 2:11** And...they saw the young child with Mary his mother, and fell down, and worshipped him: and...they presented unto him gifts; gold, and frankincense, and myrrh.

Christmas Bingo card 13

Luke 2:2	Luke 2:9	Luke 2:17	Matthew 2:8	Matthew 2:11
(And this taxing was first made when Cyrenius was governor of Syria.)	And, lo, the angel of the Lord came upon them, and the glory of the Lord shone round about them: and they were sore afraid.	And when they had seen it, they made known abroad the saying which was told them concerning this child.	And he sent them to Bethlehem, and said, Go and search diligently for the young child; and when ye have found him, bring me word again, that I may come and worship him also.	And...they saw the young child with Mary his mother, and fell down, and worshipped him: and...they presented unto him gifts; gold, and frankincense, and myrrh.
Luke 2:5	**Luke 2:13**	**Luke 2:20**	**Matthew 2:2**	**Matthew 2:14**
To be taxed with Mary his espoused wife, being great with child.	And suddenly there was with the angel a multitude of the heavenly host praising God, and saying,	And the shepherds returned, glorifying and praising God for all the things that they had heard and seen, as it was told unto them.	Saying, Where is he that is born King of the Jews? for we have seen his star in the east, and are come to worship him.	When he arose, he took the young child and his mother by night, and departed into Egypt:
Luke 2:7	**Luke 2:11**		**Matthew 2:7**	**Matthew 2:9**
And she brought forth her firstborn son, and wrapped him in swaddling clothes, and laid him in a manger; because there was no room for them in the inn.	For unto you is born this day in the city of David a Saviour, which is Christ the Lord.	*Free Space* 	Then Herod, when he had privily called the wise men, enquired of them diligently what time the star appeared.	When they had heard the king, they departed; and, lo, the star, which they saw in the east, went before them, till it came and stood over where the young child was.
Luke 2:4	**Luke 2:8**	**Luke 2:15**	**Matthew 2:3**	**Matthew 2:12**
And Joseph also went up from Galilee, out of the city of Nazareth, into Judaea, unto the city of David, which is called Bethlehem;	And there were in the same country shepherds abiding in the field, keeping watch over their flock by night.	And...the shepherds said one to another, Let us now go even unto Bethlehem, and see this thing which is come to pass, which the Lord hath made known unto us.	When Herod the king had heard these things, he was troubled, and all Jerusalem with him.	And being warned of God in a dream that they should not return to Herod, they departed into their own country another way.
Luke 2:1	**Luke 2:12**	**Luke 2:19**	**Matthew 2:5**	**Matthew 2:15**
And it came to pass in those days, that there went out a decree from Caesar Augustus, that all the world should be taxed.	And this shall be a sign unto you; Ye shall find the babe wrapped in swaddling clothes, lying in a manger.	But Mary kept all these things, and pondered them in her heart.	And they said unto him, In Bethlehem of Judaea: for thus it is written by the prophet,	And was there until the death of Herod: that it might be fulfilled which was spoken of the Lord by the prophet, saying, Out of Egypt have I called my son.

Luke 2:6	Luke 2:12	Luke 2:15	Matthew 2:7	Matthew 2:10
And so it was, that, while they were there, the days were accomplished that she should be delivered.	And this shall be a sign unto you; Ye shall find the babe wrapped in swaddling clothes, lying in a manger.	And...the shepherds said one to another, Let us now go even unto Bethlehem, and see this thing which is come to pass, which the Lord hath made known unto us.	Then Herod, when he had privily called the wise men, enquired of them diligently what time the star appeared.	When they saw the star, they rejoiced with exceeding great joy.
Luke 2:3	**Luke 2:10**	**Matthew 2:1**	**Matthew 2:4**	**Matthew 2:13**
And all went to be taxed, every one into his own city.	And the angel said unto them, Fear not: for, behold, I bring you good tidings of great joy, which shall be to all people.	Now when Jesus was born in Bethlehem of Judaea in the days of Herod the king, behold, there came wise men from the east to Jerusalem,	And when he had gathered all the chief priests and scribes of the people together, he demanded of them where Christ should be born.	The angel of the Lord appeareth to Joseph in a dream, saying, Arise, and take the young child and his mother, and flee into Egypt.
Luke 2:4	**Luke 2:8**	*Free Space*	**Matthew 2:8**	**Matthew 2:12**
And Joseph also went up from Galilee, out of the city of Nazareth, into Judaea, unto the city of David, which is called Bethlehem;	And there were in the same country shepherds abiding in the field, keeping watch over their flock by night.		And he sent them to Bethlehem, and said, Go and search diligently for the young child; and when ye have found him, bring me word again, that I may come and worship him also.	And being warned of God in a dream that they should not return to Herod, they departed into their own country another way.
Luke 2:7	**Luke 2:11**	**Luke 2:20**	**Matthew 2:5**	**Matthew 2:11**
And she brought forth her firstborn son, and wrapped him in swaddling clothes, and laid him in a manger; because there was no room for them in the inn.	For unto you is born this day in the city of David a Saviour, which is Christ the Lord.	And the shepherds returned, glorifying and praising God for all the things that they had heard and seen, as it was told unto them.	And they said unto him, In Bethlehem of Judaea: for thus it is written by the prophet,	And...they saw the young child with Mary his mother, and fell down, and worshipped him: and...they presented unto him gifts; gold, and frankincense, and myrrh.
Luke 2:5	**Luke 2:14**	**Luke 2:16**	**Matthew 2:2**	**Matthew 2:15**
To be taxed with Mary his espoused wife, being great with child.	Glory to God in the highest, and on earth peace, good will toward men.	And they came with haste, and found Mary, and Joseph, and the babe lying in a manger.	Saying, Where is he that is born King of the Jews? for we have seen his star in the east, and are come to worship him.	And was there until the death of Herod: that it might be fulfilled which was spoken of the Lord by the prophet, saying, Out of Egypt have I called my son.

JESUS

Luke 2:5 To be taxed with Mary his espoused wife, being great with child.	**Luke 2:10** And the angel said unto them, Fear not: for, behold, I bring you good tidings of great joy, which shall be to all people.	**Matthew 2:1** Now when Jesus was born in Bethlehem of Judaea in the days of Herod the king, behold, there came wise men from the east to Jerusalem,	**Matthew 2:5** And they said unto him, In Bethlehem of Judaea: for thus it is written by the prophet,	**Matthew 2:14** When he arose, he took the young child and his mother by night, and departed into Egypt:
Luke 2:7 And she brought forth her firstborn son, and wrapped him in swaddling clothes, and laid him in a manger; because there was no room for them in the inn.	**Luke 2:13** And suddenly there was with the angel a multitude of the heavenly host praising God, and saying,	**Luke 2:17** And when they had seen it, they made known abroad the saying which was told them concerning this child.	**Matthew 2:7** Then Herod, when he had privily called the wise men, enquired of them diligently what time the star appeared.	**Matthew 2:9** When they had heard the king, they departed; and, lo, the star, which they saw in the east, went before them, till it came and stood over where the young child was.
Luke 2:2 (And this taxing was first made when Cyrenius was governor of Syria.)	**Luke 2:14** Glory to God in the highest, and on earth peace, good will toward men.	 *Free Space*	**Matthew 2:8** And he sent them to Bethlehem, and said, Go and search diligently for the young child; and when ye have found him, bring me word again, that I may come and worship him also.	**Matthew 2:15** And was there until the death of Herod: that it might be fulfilled which was spoken of the Lord by the prophet, saying, Out of Egypt have I called my son.
Luke 2:3 And all went to be taxed, every one into his own city.	**Luke 2:9** And, lo, the angel of the Lord came upon them, and the glory of the Lord shone round about them: and they were sore afraid.	**Luke 2:20** And the shepherds returned, glorifying and praising God for all the things that they had heard and seen, as it was told unto them.	**Matthew 2:3** When Herod the king had heard these things, he was troubled, and all Jerusalem with him.	**Matthew 2:10** When they saw the star, they rejoiced with exceeding great joy.
Luke 2:4 And Joseph also went up from Galilee, out of the city of Nazareth, into Judaea, unto the city of David, which is called Bethlehem;	**Luke 2:11** For unto you is born this day in the city of David a Saviour, which is Christ the Lord.	**Luke 2:19** But Mary kept all these things, and pondered them in her heart.	**Matthew 2:6** And thou Bethlehem, in the land of Juda, art not the least among the princes of Juda: for out of thee shall come a Governor, that shall rule my people Israel.	**Matthew 2:12** And being warned of God in a dream that they should not return to Herod, they departed into their own country another way.

Luke 2:5 To be taxed with Mary his espoused wife, being great with child.	**Luke 2:14** Glory to God in the highest, and on earth peace, good will toward men.	**Luke 2:19** But Mary kept all these things, and pondered them in her heart.	**Matthew 2:4** And when he had gathered all the chief priests and scribes of the people together, he demanded of them where Christ should be born.	**Matthew 2:13** The angel of the Lord appeareth to Joseph in a dream, saying, Arise, and take the young child and his mother, and flee into Egypt.
Luke 2:3 And all went to be taxed, every one into his own city.	**Luke 2:13** And suddenly there was with the angel a multitude of the heavenly host praising God, and saying,	**Luke 2:20** And the shepherds returned, glorifying and praising God for all the things that they had heard and seen, as it was told unto them.	**Matthew 2:2** Saying, Where is he that is born King of the Jews? for we have seen his star in the east, and are come to worship him.	**Matthew 2:11** And...they saw the young child with Mary his mother, and fell down, and worshipped him: and...they presented unto him gifts; gold, and frankincense, and myrrh.
Luke 2:6 And so it was, that, while they were there, the days were accomplished that she should be delivered.	**Luke 2:12** And this shall be a sign unto you; Ye shall find the babe wrapped in swaddling clothes, lying in a manger.	*Free Space*	**Matthew 2:7** Then Herod, when he had privily called the wise men, enquired of them diligently what time the star appeared.	**Matthew 2:10** When they saw the star, they rejoiced with exceeding great joy.
Luke 2:2 (And this taxing was first made when Cyrenius was governor of Syria.)	**Luke 2:11** For unto you is born this day in the city of David a Saviour, which is Christ the Lord.	**Luke 2:16** And they came with haste, and found Mary, and Joseph, and the babe lying in a manger.	**Matthew 2:3** When Herod the king had heard these things, he was troubled, and all Jerusalem with him.	**Matthew 2:12** And being warned of God in a dream that they should not return to Herod, they departed into their own country another way.
Luke 2:4 And Joseph also went up from Galilee, out of the city of Nazareth, into Judaea, unto the city of David, which is called Bethlehem;	**Luke 2:10** And the angel said unto them, Fear not: for, behold, I bring you good tidings of great joy, which shall be to all people.	**Luke 2:17** And when they had seen it, they made known abroad the saying which was told them concerning this child.	**Matthew 2:8** And he sent them to Bethlehem, and said, Go and search diligently for the young child; and when ye have found him, bring me word again, that I may come and worship him also.	**Matthew 2:9** When they had heard the king, they departed; and, lo, the star, which they saw in the east, went before them, till it came and stood over where the young child was.

JESUS

Luke 2:7	Luke 2:13	Luke 2:17	Matthew 2:5	Matthew 2:10
And she brought forth her firstborn son, and wrapped him in swaddling clothes, and laid him in a manger; because there was no room for them in the inn.	And suddenly there was with the angel a multitude of the heavenly host praising God, and saying,	And when they had seen it, they made known abroad the saying which was told them concerning this child.	And they said unto him, In Bethlehem of Judaea: for thus it is written by the prophet,	When they saw the star, they rejoiced with exceeding great joy.
Luke 2:3	**Luke 2:14**	**Matthew 2:1**	**Matthew 2:2**	**Matthew 2:13**
And all went to be taxed, every one into his own city.	Glory to God in the highest, and on earth peace, good will toward men.	Now when Jesus was born in Bethlehem of Judaea in the days of Herod the king, behold, there came wise men from the east to Jerusalem,	Saying, Where is he that is born King of the Jews? for we have seen his star in the east, and are come to worship him.	The angel of the Lord appeareth to Joseph in a dream, saying, Arise, and take the young child and his mother, and flee into Egypt.
Luke 2:5	**Luke 2:11**	*Free Space*	**Matthew 2:4**	**Matthew 2:15**
To be taxed with Mary his espoused wife, being great with child.	For unto you is born this day in the city of David a Saviour, which is Christ the Lord.		And when he had gathered all the chief priests and scribes of the people together, he demanded of them where Christ should be born.	And was there until the death of Herod: that it might be fulfilled which was spoken of the Lord by the prophet, saying, Out of Egypt have I called my son.
Luke 2:4	**Luke 2:9**	**Luke 2:15**	**Matthew 2:3**	**Matthew 2:9**
And Joseph also went up from Galilee, out of the city of Nazareth, into Judaea, unto the city of David, which is called Bethlehem;	And, lo, the angel of the Lord came upon them, and the glory of the Lord shone round about them: and they were sore afraid.	And...the shepherds said one to another, Let us now go even unto Bethlehem, and see this thing which is come to pass, which the Lord hath made known unto us.	When Herod the king had heard these things, he was troubled, and all Jerusalem with him.	When they had heard the king, they departed; and, lo, the star, which they saw in the east, went before them, till it came and stood over where the young child was.
Luke 2:2	**Luke 2:10**	**Luke 2:18**	**Matthew 2:8**	**Matthew 2:12**
(And this taxing was first made when Cyrenius was governor of Syria.)	And the angel said unto them, Fear not: for, behold, I bring you good tidings of great joy, which shall be to all people.	And all they that heard it wondered at those things which were told them by the shepherds.	And he sent them to Bethlehem, and said, Go and search diligently for the young child; and when ye have found him, bring me word again, that I may come and worship him also.	And being warned of God in a dream that they should not return to Herod, they departed into their own country another way.

Candy canes jigsaw puzzle—Color and cut the candy canes into puzzle shapes, and then put them together again.

Santa jigsaw puzzle—Color and cut Santa into puzzle shapes, and then put him together again.

Answer Keys to the Word Finds
and Crossword Puzzles

(See pages 128–30 and 135–37.)

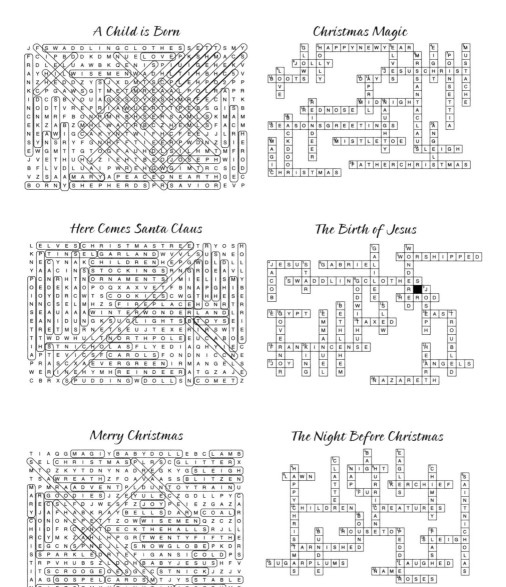

A Child is Born

Christmas Magic

Here Comes Santa Claus

The Birth of Jesus

Merry Christmas

The Night Before Christmas

Chapter Twelve
Holiday Traditions

*C*hristmas is a holiday steeped in tradition. Decorating a Christmas tree, giving and receiving gifts, caroling, and participating in a pageant are just a few. If you use your imagination, you can come up with several fun and original ideas with which to start your own traditions. Here are a few suggestions, along with some blank spaces to add your own ideas.

1. Create or purchase gifts together as a family.

    Gifts can be colored pictures, poems that family members have written, or crafts that little hands have created. Anything given with thought, care, and love will be appreciated, and your children will truly learn that it is better to give than to receive.

    Christmas shopping together can also be fun. Before you leave home to go to the store, discuss with your children how much money can be spent. Invite gift suggestions, and once you get to the store, stick to your budget.

2. Choose a family or an individual who is struggling financially or emotionally, and anonymously fill their needs. This not only includes those individuals in homeless shelters and hospitals, but it also includes family members or neighbors who are struggling.

3. Volunteer to serve in a homeless shelter, soup kitchen, hospital, or care center.

4. Buy family members new pajamas or nightgowns each year to wear on Christmas Eve. Wear special attire on Christmas Day. Remember to take a lot of pictures to preserve the memories.

5. On Christmas Eve, read the story of the Savior's birth in Luke 2 and Matthew 2.

6. Light a candle at midnight on Christmas Eve for those less fortunate. Say a prayer for those in need and for an end to all human suffering.

7. Fully decorate your tree before Christmas, except for the top branch. Make it a yearly ritual to add a star or an angel to the top of the tree on Christmas Eve.

8. Read a Christmas story every night in December until Christmas Eve, and then read from the Bible the story of the Savior's birth.

9. Make it a Christmas tradition to read "The Night Before Christmas" by Clement Moore.

10. If your family is becoming too large to buy gifts for everyone, draw names so that each person only has to buy one nice gift.

11. Place a call to a family member who is away from home for the holidays. Out-of-town relatives would also appreciate the gesture.

12. Buy Christmas ornaments for babies who were born within the last twelve months.

13. Open one gift each on Christmas Eve.

14. Allow your children to enjoy Santa Claus when they are young. Although they will someday stop believing in him, they will never forget the magic or lose the spirit of Christmas.

15. Practice random acts of charity. You can never be too kind.

16. Go for a drive and view local Christmas lights and decorations.

17. Serve the same favorite meal every Christmas Eve, have a special breakfast together every Christmas morning, and plan on the same out-of-the-ordinary dinner each Christmas Day.

18. Go caroling as a family each year, and don't forget to sing carols on Christmas Eve.

19. Buy or create an advent calendar and count down the days until Christmas. (See page 22.)

20. Have each member of your family create a wish list. Even if they don't get what they want, it's still fun to dream, and it will give others an idea of what each family member would like for Christmas.

21. Use antique or special ornaments and decorations each year.

22. Participate in a Christmas Eve graveside candlelight ceremony. (See page 74.)

23. Decorate a loved one's grave. (See page 73.)

24. Buy each family member a special Christmas mug and enjoy hot chocolate together on Christmas Eve and Christmas night. Don't forget to light a fire in the fireplace!

25. Join a choir or participate in a Christmas play.
26. Write letters to missionaries, servicemen or women, care center residents, hospital patients, or anyone else who needs to be remembered during the holidays.
27. Watch a special Christmas movie as a family.

28. _____

_____

29. _____

_____

30. _____

_____

31. _____

_____

32. _____

_____

33. _____

_____

34. _____

_____

35. _____

_____

36. _____

_____

37. _____

_____

38. _____

_____

39. _____

_____

40. _____

_____

Chapter Thirteen
To Light His Way:
The Beauty of Luminaries

Luminaries can be warm, beautiful, and inviting. According to modern legend, luminaries were first used to light the Savior's way to the homes of his faithful saints on Christmas Eve.

Materials

Colored or plain paper bags
Sand, kitty litter, rock salt, or rocks
Votive or tea light candles
Measuring cup
Lighter

Optional (for decorating luminaries)

Patterns at the end of this chapter
Crayons or markers (if children are to be involved)
X-acto knife and decorative-edged scissors
Glitter
Glue
Spray paint
Aluminum foil

Directions

If desired, decorate your luminaries before lighting them. If you want colored bags, visit your local craft store. You can also spray paint plain paper bags, or color them with crayons or markers. Remember that the glow of the candle needs to be able to shine through the sides of the bag, so keep your decorations light.

Create your own designs or use the patterns on the following pages. Cookie cutters can also be used to trace patterns on the sides of the bags. (See pages 93–102 for more patterns.) The patterns can be traced onto the paper bags, colored, or cut out with an X-acto knife or scissors. Once the luminary is lit, the light shines through the cutout patterns and creates a soft, glowing shadow on the sidewalk and nearby objects.

If you want your luminary to be extra bright, line the back side of the paper bag with aluminum foil (shiny side out) before adding the sand. The luminaries in the photo are lined with aluminum foil.

The patterns look difficult to cut out, but if you use the right tool, it will only take a few minutes. X-acto knives are inexpensive and seem to do the best job. (See photo.) For safety reasons, children should not be allowed to use an X-acto knife.

To cut out the patterns, place the pattern inside the sack and firmly trace along the figures with the blade of the X-act knife. Press hard enough to cut through the top layer of the sack.

Once you have prepared your luminaries, decide where you want to display them (usually along a path or a sidewalk).

After you have placed your bags, fill them with approximately 2 cups of sand, kitty litter, rock salt, or rocks until each bag has at least a 2-inch base.

Securely twist a candle into the sand in the middle of each bag.

As it begins to grow dark, carefully light each candle. For safety reasons, children should not be allowed to light the candles.

Enjoy the beauty and ambiance of your luminaries!

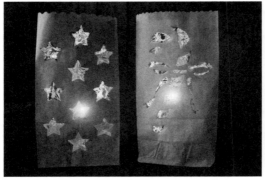 

Luminaries   X-acto knife

Candy cane luminary

Wreath and
star luminaries

Stars luminary

Christmas trees
luminary

Chapter Fourteen
Enjoy the Magic of the Holidays:
The Symbols of Christmas

Santa Claus has been a controversial figure for years, especially in some Christian circles. He has his place in our holiday celebrations, however, and even though some of us don't always agree with the commercialism he represents, we can still enjoy the same magical feeling we had for him when we were children. Maybe we can't completely remove him from our holiday celebrations, but with a little understanding, we might at least be able to reach a compromise.

According to Webster's Dictionary, a symbol is something that represents or stands for something else. Let's begin with the color of Santa's suit. The color red is symbolic, just as most of our Christmas traditions are.

The Color Red

Red is the dominant color of Christmas. It is a symbol of the Savior's blood that was shed for us. Christ gave his life so that all men who were willing to keep his commandments would have eternal life. Red is deep, intense, and vivid. It is the symbol of the great sacrifice Jesus Christ and our Heavenly Father made for us. Tradition states that Santa is symbolic of the Savior himself. How can this be? For starters, Santa's suit is red, and he does nothing but give good gifts to those who are worthy. Does this sound familiar?

The Star of Bethlehem

The star of Bethlehem was a heavenly sign of promise. God promised us a Savior, and the brilliant star of the east was a sure sign of that promise.

The star now symbolizes God's love for mankind. It also reminds us that God's promises are always fulfilled.

The Evergreen Tree

The evergreen's pure green color is maintained all year around. Green is the youthful, hopeful, and abundant color of nature. All the needles on an evergreen tree point upward, symbolic of man's thoughts toward heaven. This great green tree has been a friend to mankind since the beginning of the world. It has sheltered him, warmed him, and given him beauty.

Bells

As lost sheep are found by the sound of their bells, so should bells ring for the lost souls of men. Bells symbolize the guiding hand of the greatest shepherd of all time—Jesus Christ. They remind us that we are all precious in the sight of our Heavenly Father.

Candles

The candle is man's symbol of the star of Bethlehem. The candle's small light reflects the brilliance of a greater light from long ago. Candles were once placed on the Christmas tree. They were like little glowing stars in the night sky, shining through the dark green boughs of the evergreen. Safety has now replaced the candles with pretty twinkling lights that still continue to remind us of the birth of the Savior.

Bows

Bows are placed on our gifts to remind us of the brotherhood of man. We should remember that as a bow is tied together, so should all mankind be tied together. We should be bound together in unity and love, with good will toward all men.

Gifts

The brightly wrapped Christmas gift symbolizes our Heavenly Father's love for us. He gave us the gift of his Son, Jesus Christ, and in turn, Jesus gave his life that we might live again.

Candy Canes

The candy cane represents the shepherd's crook. The crook on the end of a sheepherder's staff was used to pull strayed sheep back into the fold.

The candy cane is a reminder that we are all our brother's keeper, and once again, we must never forget that the greatest shepherd of all, Jesus Christ, is the Son of the living God.

Wreaths

The wreath symbolizes the eternal nature of love. It never ceases, never stops, and never ends. Life is eternal, and if we obey the commandments of God, we will live forever in his presence with our loved ones.

Chapter Fifteen
"If Ye Have Done It unto the Least of These"
Volunteerism and Service

The Lord spent his entire life in the service of others. He did so much for us, and yet we do so little in return. He asked us to love one another, but how many of us truly love our neighbor?

And who is our neighbor? The Lord made that clear when he related the parable of the Good Samaritan. He said, "Which now of these three, thinkest thou, was neighbour unto him that fell among the thieves? And he [the lawyer] said, He that shewed mercy on him. Then said Jesus unto him, Go, and do thou likewise" (Luke 10:36–37).

Serving others can be gratifying, and, for the most part, it doesn't take that much effort. A smile, a kind word, a listening ear, or an understanding heart can go a long way. The ability to reach out to others is a blessing in itself, for when we are mindful of others, we not only bless their lives, but we also bless our own.

Homeless Shelters and Soup Kitchens

Opportunities to serve are all around us. Phone books are an excellent source of locating shelters and soup kitchens, and so is the Internet. Here are a few links to websites that can provide you with information about volunteering. Keep in mind that these websites change from time to time, especially around the holidays, so it's best to search the web to find updated information.

http://www.ehow.com/how_10121_volunteer-soup-kitchen.html
http://www.ehow.com/how_10120_donate-food-soup.html
http://www.hud.gov/local/index.cfm?state=ut&topic=homeless

http://www.artistshelpingchildren.org/shelters.html
http://www.findlocalshelter.info/homeless_shelters.htm

Reputable Charities

If you want to donate to a charity, make sure it's a reputable one. The following websites have good advice on how to find charities you can trust. Again, it is recommended that you do a web search each year to find the most recent information.

http://www.bankrate.com/brm/news/advice/20020107a.asp
http://people.howstuffworks.com/philanthropy1.htm
http://www.charitywatch.org/toprated.html
http://www.usafreedomcorps.gov/about_usafc/newsroom/
    announcements_dynamic.asp?ID=840
http://systemagicmotives.com/Charities/Charities.htm

Guess Who?
Anonymously Make Someone's Christmas Brighter

Several years ago, back in the early sixties, my father was temporarily laid off from his job. The layoff didn't last long, but, unfortunately, it happened just a few weeks before Christmas.

My parents handled the situation beautifully. My mother made us Raggedy Ann and Andy dolls, and we were each given a homemade stocking with a package of M&Ms® in it. It was a special time, because even though we didn't have much, we knew we were loved.

But that was only the beginning. When we opened the door to see if it had snowed during the night, we found two large boxes filled with food, toys, and goodies on our porch. I had never seen so many toys in my life! I remember the tears in my parents' eyes, and I remember their prayers of gratitude for weeks, months, and even years afterward.

I know God has reserved special blessings for those who bring joy into the lives of others. It doesn't take much time or effort on the part of the benefactor, but it means a lot to the recipient.

Take the time to serve others this holiday season. You'll be glad you did!

Chapter Sixteen
The Reason We Celebrate Christmas:
The Birth of Our Savior, Jesus Christ

When I was a child, I was chosen to play the part of the mother of Jesus in our church's Christmas pageant. Even at the young age of four, it was an honor for me to take Mary's place beside Joseph and hold the baby Jesus in my arms.

My mother created a simple costume for me out of an old sheet. (See the nativity costume pattern on page 180.) Using a sheet for a costume doesn't sound too appealing, but the finished product looked authentic. I was allowed to bring my favorite doll to church to play the part of Jesus, but my happiest moment was when I learned I didn't have to memorize any lines. A narrator read from Luke 2:1–20 and Matthew 2:1–15, and each of us participating in the pageant enacted our parts as the narrator read the account of Christ's birth.

It is always nice to use the Bible itself to narrate the story of the birth of the Savior; however, it is not always convenient. Because of this, I have included the verses from Luke and Matthew here for you to copy. I've also suggested Christmas carols that can be sung throughout the narrative, and you can find the lyrics to these songs in chapter 10 on page 104.

May you have the best Christmas pageant ever!

The First Christmas: A Nativity Pageant for Children

Narrator: When Adam and Eve were cast out of the Garden of Eden, they were promised that someday Jesus would come to earth as our Savior. He would give his life for us. All the prophets since the beginning of time foretold Christ's birth, and they rejoiced and looked forward to it.

The night of Jesus' birth finally arrived, and what a glorious night it was! Let us all join in celebration of the first Christmas!

Song: "Joy to the World"

Narrator: "And it came to pass in those days, that there went out a decree from Caesar Augustus, that all the world should be taxed. (And this taxing was first made when Cyrenius was governor of Syria.) And all went to be taxed, every one into his own city. And Joseph also went up from Galilee, out of the city of Nazareth, into Judaea, unto the city of David, which is called Bethlehem; (because he was of the house and lineage of David:) To be taxed with Mary his espoused wife, being great with child."

Song: "O Little Town of Bethlehem"

Narrator: "And so it was, that, while they were there, the days were accomplished that she should be delivered. And she brought forth her firstborn son, and wrapped him in swaddling clothes, and laid him in a manger; because there was no room for them in the inn."

Song: "Away in a Manger"

Narrator: "And there were in the same country shepherds abiding in the field, keeping watch over their flock by night. And, lo, the angel of the Lord came upon them, and the glory of the Lord shone round about them: and they were sore afraid. And the angel said unto them, Fear not: for, behold, I bring you good tidings of great joy, which shall be to all people. For unto you is born this day in the city of David a Saviour, which is Christ the Lord. And this shall be a sign unto you; Ye shall find the babe wrapped in swaddling clothes, lying in a manger. And suddenly there was with the angel a multitude of the heavenly host praising God, and saying, Glory to God in the highest, and on earth peace, good will toward men."

Song: "Hark, the Herald Angels Sing"

Narrator: "And it came to pass, as the angels were gone away from them into heaven, the shepherds said one to another, Let us now go even unto Bethlehem, and see this thing which is come to pass, which the Lord hath made known unto us. And they came with haste, and found Mary, and Joseph, and the babe lying in a manger."

Song: "Oh, Come All Ye Faithful"

Narrator: "And when they had seen it, they made known abroad the saying which was told them concerning this child. And all they that heard it wondered at those things which were told them by the shepherds. But Mary kept all these things, and pondered them in her heart. And the shepherds returned, glorifying and praising God for all the things that they had heard and seen, as it was told unto them.

"Now when Jesus was born in Bethlehem of Judaea in the days of Herod the king, behold, there came wise men from the east to Jerusalem, Saying, Where is he that is born King of the Jews? for we have seen his star in the east, and are come to worship him."

Song: "We Three Kings"

Narrator: "When Herod the king had heard these things, he was troubled, and all Jerusalem with him. And when he had gathered all the chief priests and scribes of the people together, he demanded of them where Christ should be born. And they said unto him, In Bethlehem of Judaea: for thus it is written by the prophet, And thou Bethlehem, in the land of Juda, art not the least among the princes of Juda: for out of thee shall come a Governor, that shall rule my people Israel."

Song: "O Come, O Come, Emmanuel"

Narrator: "Then Herod, when he had privily called the wise men, enquired of them diligently what time the star appeared. And he sent them to Bethlehem, and said, Go and search diligently for the young child; and when ye have found him, bring me word again, that I may come and worship him also. When they had heard the king, they departed; and, lo, the star, which they saw in the east, went before them, till it came and stood over where the young child was. When they saw the star, they rejoiced with exceeding great joy. And when they were come into the house, they saw the young child with Mary his mother, and fell down, and worshipped him: and when they had opened their treasures, they presented unto him gifts; gold, and frankincense, and myrrh."

Song: "What Child Is This?"

Narrator: And so it was that Christ was born in Bethlehem on that sacred night so long ago. Angels proclaimed his birth, and humble shepherds heeded their song. Wise men sought him then, and wise men seek him now.

Song: "Silent Night"

Basic Nativity Costume

Creating a costume for a Christmas pageant doesn't have to be difficult. Sometimes the simpler it is, the better. Putting something together can be a lot of fun—that is, if it doesn't become a burden.

For a basic costume, place a towel on your child's head and wrap a cloth belt around it. Dress him in a robe and send him out on stage. If you have the time and are willing to put forth the effort, however, there is another way to do it.

When my mother made my costume from an old sheet, she cut a long piece of fabric that gradually tapered out toward the ends. There were two small rectangles on each side for my arms. The fabric was a little more than twice the length of my height, which was measured from the bone at the base of the back of my neck down to the floor. Mother also measured the circumference of my arms and the width of my body and added enough extra material so I could move and walk. Her measurements were not exact, and yours don't need to be either.

Mary Elizabeth Stuart dressed as the Mother of Jesus.

Just make sure the costume will fit your child comfortably. He is better off if it is too large rather than too small.

A T-shaped hole was cut for the neckline, which allowed me to easily slip my head through the opening. I wore the cut in back and pinned it shut. If the cut isn't too long, it can be worn in front, which gives the costume the appearance of having a collar. If you don't want to pin the costume, you can always use Velcro®.

My mother folded the piece of fabric in half at the sleeves and sewed the two side seams. No hems were necessary because she used pinking sheers. (The pinking sheers made it so the edges didn't tear as easily.) If you plan on using the costume for more than a year, you'll want to hem the edges or bind them with bias binding. Iron-on adhesives are also available, such as Stitch Witchery and HeatnBond by Therm O Web.

The head covering was the length and width of my height and was held in place by a strip of fabric tied around my head. The head piece doesn't have to be that large. If there hadn't been enough fabric left in the sheet, my mother probably would have cut it smaller.

As a finishing touch, a long strip of fabric was cut from the sheet and tied around my waist.

This simple pattern will work for any of the nativity costumes, and for your convenience, I have included a smaller version of it on the following page. Adding homemade accessories, such as a shepherd's staff, cardboard wings, a pipe cleaner halo, or a decorated paper crown (using beads or glass gems from your local craft store), will make the costume complete.

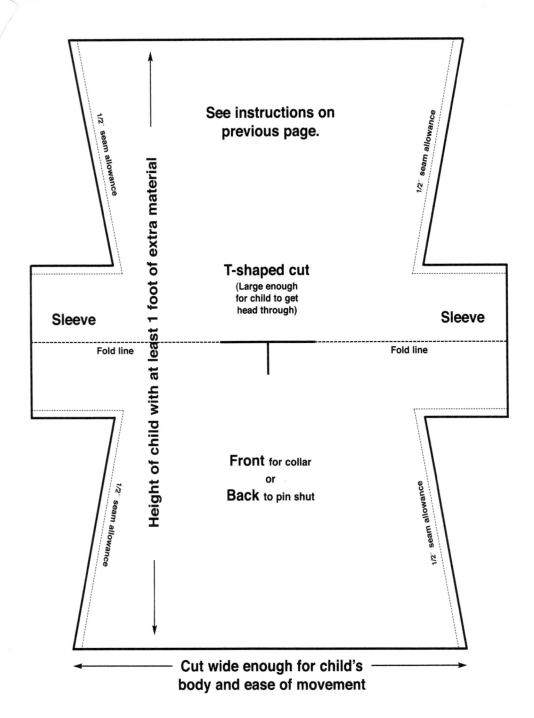

See instructions on previous page.

Height of child with at least 1 foot of extra material

1/2" seam allowance

1/2" seam allowance

T-shaped cut
(Large enough for child to get head through)

Sleeve

Sleeve

Fold line

Fold line

Front for collar
or
Back to pin shut

1/2" seam allowance

1/2" seam allowance

Cut wide enough for child's body and ease of movement

Nativity costume